GW00703094

Stolen Innocence

The True-Life Terror I Experienced as a Child

By

Elaine Carole

Copyright © 2007 by Elaine Carole

All rights reserved. No part of this book shall be repro-duced or transmitted in any form or by any means, electronic, mechanical, magnetic, photographic including photocopying, recording or by any information storage and retrieval system, without prior written permission of the publisher. No patent liability is assumed with respect to the use of the information contained herein. Although every precaution has been taken in the preparation of this book, the publisher and author assume no responsibility for errors or omissions. Neither is any liability assumed for damages resulting from the use of the information contained herein.

ISBN 0-7414-3917-4

Published by:

INFINITY
PUBLISHING.COM

1094 New DeHaven Street, Suite 100
West Conshohocken, PA 19428-2713
Info@buybooksontheweb.com
www.buybooksontheweb.com
Toll-free (877) BUY BOOK
Local Phone (610) 941-9999
Fax (610) 941-9959

Printed in the United States of America

Printed on Recycled Paper

Published March 2007

Introduction

I am sharing this story because I want other victims, or potential victims, to know that sexual abuse is not their fault. They should not be ashamed or afraid of telling other loved ones that a child molester is victimizing them. In fact, they should notify an adult they trust as soon as possible to avoid the possible victimization of other individuals, especially children.

On the outside, it appeared that I lived the perfect little childhood in the perfect little home. In reality, I was living a nightmare night after night and day after day. What I experienced for almost ten years is something no little girl, or boy for that matter, should have to experience. Children are innocent; my innocence was stolen from me and it is something that can never be replaced. I wish everyday now that I would have told someone earlier. I realize now that I wasn't being fair to myself, nor too many others. I should have taken the risk and exposed the hurtful monster that essentially ruined my life years ago. Instead, my silence allowed this monster to continue violating other innocent children and robbing them of their innocence also. I share this with you in hopes that if you or someone you love is being robbed as I was, they will be encouraged to come forward to take the steps necessary to get the monster off the street.

Finally, I am sharing my story because people need to realize that this type of abuse goes on in all types of homes. You might be poor, or you might be from an upper-class family; you might be an only child, or you might have several brothers or sisters. The abuser could be a stepfather or a natural father; he could be an uncle, stepbrother, or even a family friend. In any case, molestation and rape "affection" as my stepfather called them are wrong. I was not going to come forward and share my story with the police let alone the court system, but I had no choice. Many may think I did, but when the monster I grew up with was violating other children, choice became something that was not an option.

My other intension for this book is for mothers, fathers, sisters, brothers, friends, aunts, uncles, cousins, etc… to read this and make themselves more aware of their families and their relationships with one another. "Not in my family" or "that would never happen to me" invites a violator to strip you of your dreams, your desires, and most importantly your innocence. By being aware and alert, you might help avert the devastating effects of sexual abuse.

Because of the sensitive nature of this factual account, I have changed the names of all involved. Keep in mind some of the contents may be sensitive in nature.

Dedication

I am dedicating this book to my best friend, my mother. She is the most understanding and caring person I know. She opened her heart and soul to me in my greatest time of need. I will never be able to repay her--not that she would expect me to, but I will forever be grateful to her. I know that I am very lucky to have such a wonderful person in my life and, I now know that we should not take each day for granted. Since the trial, I have learned to appreciate life and what it has to offer.

Mom, thank you for being you and thanks for holding my hand and crying with me when I felt so alone and scared. I love you.

Chapter One – I Have a Secret

The words "The jury is in and they have a verdict" rang through the dark halls of the courthouse. Those words will forever ring in my ears. "What are they going to say? Do they believe me, or do they believe the defendant?" These questions raged through my mind as I pulled myself together and mustered up the nerve and will to enter the courtroom; the place where I felt my future was going to be determined.

Thinking back now, I always thought of myself as a happy and strong type of person. I am a single mother and have had my fair share of challenges of everyday life. Little did I know the lengths to which my happiness and strength would be further challenged following a phone call to my mother one day from the local police department. In a nutshell, my world crashed around me.

The call was from a Sergeant Chris Long. Sgt. Long wanted to meet with my mother regarding her ex-husband, the man who had been my stepfather. My mother, of course, was curious and wondered what Sgt. Long could want from her.

"What is this about, Sgt. Long? I haven't seen or talked with Paul for over fifteen years," my mother, Liz, responded.

"This is a matter that I would rather not discuss over the phone with you, Ms. Carole. When could we meet?" Sgt. Long replied.

They both agreed to meet the next evening at 7:00. My mother and I sat that night trying to figure out what it could be. Did he do something to his wife, Betty? It wouldn't be far-fetched since Paul had a temper that was known to get out of hand. Deep down I felt I knew what it was, and the feeling in my stomach was more than I could handle. That night I didn't sleep. My mind was going crazy and fear was coming over me.

The next day, I tried hard to concentrate on my work and prepare for that evening, which was to attend school. I was glad I had a class that evening and would not have to face the police with the questions I knew they would ask.

My mother called me on my work phone. "I know what the police want to talk to me about," my mother said.

"What?" I said.

"I got a call at the office from a neighbor of Paul's. She said that Paul is being investigated for child molestation. Can you believe that? Apparently he has been doing some pretty horrible things to the children in the neighborhood."

My ears were throbbing and I could barely control myself. Thank god she was telling me this over the phone.

"I told the woman that I was meeting with the police this evening but didn't know why until now. My god Elaine could Paul be capable of such a horrible crime?"

"I don't know, mom. It's been a lot of years so, I guess anything is possible." That was the only response I could think of to say. I felt the tears building up in my eyes and my heart had a horrible burning feeling inside.

I went to school that night not hearing a word the professor was saying. I sat in the classroom just watching the clock and wondering what was going on with my mother and the police. What was he saying? Was he asking about me? Did she think I knew anything about it?

It was time for a fifteen-minute break at school. I held my cell phone in my hand with the phone number programmed in it for what felt like forever before pushing the send button. My mother answered the phone but sounded extremely professional, as if someone was there with her. I asked how things were going, and she said fine but that Sgt. Long and she were still talking. I told her I would call her on my next break and hung up. I felt a little relief after hanging up with her. She didn't sound emotional or worked up, like she knew something.

I went back to class and continued to watch the clock until the next break. When it finally came, I called home and my mother answered the phone in a more relaxed manner.

"So what did the police have to say? Was that woman correct this morning saying Paul had done some horrible things to children in the neighborhood?" I asked.

"Yes, apparently he's been investigated for several years. Charges were brought up against him but they never stuck, so he's gotten away with this. Listen I'll fill you in on everything when you get home. What time are you getting out tonight?" asked my mother.

"I will be home by 10:00. I guess I should get back to class now, so I'll see you then." I hung up. My chest felt tight, and I wanted in the worst way to leave class but wasn't sure I wanted to leave to go home.

Class ended a little earlier than usual. The ride home was quick as the school is less than five minutes from home. I took a few extra side roads home, hoping to hit a few more red lights, but traffic was light and I seemed to get home even quicker than normal.

When I walked in the house my mother seemed fine. She asked all the usual questions about class. I changed my clothes as usual and even got my dinner, the whole time watching mom and noticing that she seemed okay. Relief settled over me. As I sat at the table to eat, I said, "Well, tell me everything. What has Paul done now?"

"Well, it seems that Paul has been a very bad man. Back as early as 1993; he was accused of touching a little girl in an inappropriate manner, and got away with it. Then he did it again but this time to a couple of little girls about a year and a half ago. He was arrested, but the state couldn't get a conviction because the two little girls seemed to have stories that weren't one hundred percent the same. So the charges were dropped. Sgt. Long's superior has been receiving a lot of calls from the mothers in the neighborhood about Paul. He's been taking pictures of the kids as they ride their bikes and even following some of them as they walk to school. Long's superior told him the case is back open and wants him to talk to everyone in Paul's life whether they're from the present or the past."

My only response was "wow"; I had that feeling again that my worst fears were going to come true. My secret was going to come out.

We both sat in silence just looking at one another. My mother had such a look of disbelief. She said, "You know, if Sgt. Long would have told me that he killed someone or hurt his wife, it wouldn't have been such a shock as this. I can't believe he would do this. I mean, I believe it, but I just *can't* believe it. Long wanted me to talk to both you and your brother to see if either of you knew anything. I told him that you two would have told me, but he asked that I talk to you anyway. He did seem rather interested in you when he found out that he had adopted you. So, Elaine did Paul ever do anything to you that you never told me?"

I quickly responded "no" but could not look her in the eye.

Mom seemed to believe me though. The one thing about my relationship with my mother is that we are both open and honest. We share everything—well, in this case, almost everything. How could I tell her this after all these years? My goal had always been to protect her and my brother from this horrible secret. Now there was that chance it could come out--something I had never thought of. I never believed Paul would do this to a *stranger*. I thought it was just one of those things, and, once I was gone, his disgusting fetish would go away.

A day or two passed, and my mother paid a visit to my brother and his wife. Mom told them everything about Paul and her long visit with Sgt. Long. My brother harbored a lot of hurt and anger towards Paul, who was very mentally and emotionally abusive towards my brother when he was growing up. He always told my brother he was stupid and would never amount to anything. Of course my brother and his wife were sad to hear about the children and full of anger towards Paul for doing such an unspeakable crime.

Days went by and I began to feel more and more relief that I was in the clear. I figured that since my mother spoke to both of us and neither one of us had any information to

4

offer, it was over and I could go back to my well-guarded life. I was wrong though. It was only the beginning.

One day the phone rang. It was Sgt. Long. "Well hello Elaine. I was hoping that the two of us could sit down and talk for a while. I believe you have information that could be critical to the case. When could we meet?"

I had to think quickly. "I'm going out of town for work and won't be back for several days. What I can do though is call you while I'm away so we can set something up."

He said that was fine and we ended our call. Of course that was far from the truth. I had no plan to return his call.

While in my hotel room, I did a lot of thinking and the one thought that kept coming back to me over and over again was that I survived this terror. I was fine and these kids would be fine, too. But as many times as that thought came to me, another thought also kept coming back. "What if these children are not as strong as I was and this ruins their lives forever? Can I live with that? NO!" Needless to say, during that trip I didn't get a whole lot of rest. I thought a lot about the children and my life as a child. My childhood was a lie. Everyday was a performance; I was the perfect little daughter in the perfect little home. It was a very draining life, always feeling on guard and always fearful at night. It wasn't fair, and I decided if I could help others avoid what I experienced, then I really need to talk to Sgt. Long.

During the second night, I started to jot things down on paper. I wrote down such things as who would be hurt by my coming forward, and who would benefit from it. I experienced a lot of emotions while doing this. I kept that paper for the next day and a half and then, while I was at the airport lounge, I read over it one more time and threw it away. While trying to relax in the lounge area, I began to think that maybe something had happened while I was away and I wouldn't need to talk to the police after all. Deep down though, I knew that wasn't true, but I was holding on to any hope possible. It was time to board the plane. Once on the flight, I tried to relax. It was going to be a long flight, and at this point, there was nothing I could do. I put on my headset and tuned to some relaxing music, and let my mind drift. Normally I can drift off into a light sleep when I fly, but this time it was as if a slide projector was flashing pictures into my head. I was getting flashes of things I experienced as a child, I was picturing my mothers face once I told her, I was even picturing the children in Paul's neighborhood, not that I knew what they looked like, but I was imagining them to look like I did, little girl with pig-tails and skinned knees from falling off my bike all the time. Eventually I was able to just listen to the music and clear my mind of the horrible slide show going on in my head.

When I returned home, I wasn't in the house for more than ten minutes when the phone rang. It was Sgt. Long on the other end. "Elaine, I didn't hear from you. When can we meet? It's very important to the case."

I blurted out, "Tomorrow at 12:00. My house would be good."

"Great. I'll see you then," replied Long.

I hung up the phone and looked in the mirror, asking myself out loud, "What the hell did you just do?" I felt sick all afternoon. Of course, I didn't sleep at all that night. I more or less made up my mind at that point what needed to be done. Now all I had to do was wait until 12:00 the next day.

Chapter Two – The Meeting

The morning was the same as usual. I made my son breakfast while he got ready for school. After he left, I did my usual thing: got myself a shower did my hair, and, since I work from home, I was able to put on my shorts and T-shirt. I started my job as usual about 8:30 and did my normal routine. I e-mailed my boss and told him that I had an appointment and would not be available for a couple of hours around noon.

At about 11:30 a sick feeling came over me, and I decided to take my dog outside for a little walk. I needed to clear my head and prepare for what was about to happen. Promptly at 12:00, Sgt. Long was at my front door, and when the doorbell rang my heart went into my throat. I opened the door.

"Hello. My name is Sgt. Chris Long. It's finally nice to meet you. I hope your trip was a good one."

"Nice to meet you, too, Sgt. Long, and yes my trip was good, but as always, it's nice to be home."

"Please, call me Chris."

We made a lot of small talk about my son and my dog that was excited to have someone new in the house.

I invited Chris into the living room and then offered him a soft drink. My office phone rang, and he asked if I needed to get it. I told him it was fine that I would let the voicemail get it.

After we discussed what I did for a living, Sgt. Long set his drink down. "Well, Elaine, you know why I'm here. I know your mother told you about the things Paul has been doing in the neighborhood. I want you to know that I will not be taping this. I want our conversation to be relaxed and if I need to, I'll just write some things down."

"Well, before you go any further, let me just tell you everything before I lose my nerve. Then, if you have any questions, you can ask them after. Would that be okay?"

"That's fine, Elaine. However you want to do this and whatever makes you more comfortable is fine with me."

"I don't know if it makes me more comfortable. I just need to get this off my chest before I have a heart attack." I took a deep breath and remember sitting in silence for a moment. "I know that you heard that Paul adopted me when I was very small. I was probably about the age of three. My mother divorced my natural father when I was a lot younger than that. She met Paul and they fell in love. After they were married in May of 1970, Paul wanted to adopt me. My natural father was more or less talked into signing rights over allowing Paul to adopt me. My natural father's relatives convinced him that it would be best for me and that Paul would be a wonderful provider to both my mother and me.

"I had no idea that the man raising me was not my 'real' father until one summer evening when I was about seven years old. I know it must have been summer because at that time, I was wearing baby-doll pj's to bed, and living up north where it's cold, it had to be summer. My mother came into my room with an envelope in her hand. We sat together on my bed. I had the prettiest room ever. The bedspread was purple and white squares with white frilly lace along the bottom. On my bed I had a beautiful doll that had a huge dress that draped over the bed. My mother said she had something she wanted and needed to share with me now that I was a big girl. She proceeded to tell me about her marriage to Paul and how it was not her first marriage. She explained that a long time ago, she was married to another man named Rick. Rick was a great man, but they were not meant to be married. She shared in a loving manner how some people just don't belong together and how it's best that they separate and live new lives where they can be happier like she was with Paul.

"With that said, she then pulled out photos from the envelope. She showed me the pictures of her and Rick along with friends that were part of the wedding. She pointed out Rick and held my hand and said that he was my 'real' father. I must have had a look of disbelief because she just seemed to lean in closer and hold my hand a little firmer. She explained that he loved me very much but knew that Paul loved me as well, and he would be a wonderful provider and father to me. I remember staring at the photos thinking how beautiful my mother looked in her long white dress and how handsome my father looked. They both looked happy together. It was hard to believe that the man downstairs was not my father. Everyone always said how much I looked like him. After all, we both had the same hair color and our eyes seemed to match. We were even both left-handed.

"My mother and I sat there a little longer she was very concerned about my well-being. She told me she loved me and asked if I wanted to keep these photos, which of course, I did. After she left, I remember going to my mirror and holding the photo next to my face. I looked at myself then the photo and back again. I then put them back in the envelope for safekeeping.

"Shortly after that, Paul knocked on my door and came in. He had tears in his eyes and a quiver in his voice. He bent down and kissed me on the cheek. He asked if I was okay and I said 'yes.' He then sat beside me and told me that he felt very lucky to have me as his daughter. Then the conversation took a different turn. He went from the loving concerned dad to something a little deeper. He told me about how expensive it was to adopt me and all the legal work involved. He also told me a different story than my mother. He told me that Rick did not love me and how he was mean to my mother and me, but now we were going to be safe with him.

"He then shared with me how our relationship as father and daughter was going to be even more special than my friend Colleen and her father. We were special and we had a closer bond, one no one would ever be able to share or have. While saying these things to me, he then took my envelope of the photos, opened it up, and took out the pictures. I told him that mom had given it to me. He said that I didn't need to have pictures of a man that didn't love or care for me. If he did, he would have fought for me and would not have

9

given me up the way he did. He ripped them up and threw them in the trash, then kissed me rather hard on the lips before leaving my room.

"Once he left, I took the photos from the trash and put them back in the envelope so that later I could tape them back together. I put them under my mattress where I thought they would be safe and well hidden. I was wrong. When I went back to get them, the envelope and photos were gone, never to be seen again."

"Wow, Elaine, that's a lot of information for a little girl to handle in one day. That must have been overwhelming," said Sgt. Long.

"You know, Chris that was nothing. I thought it was a lot, but what was to come later was where the ultimate nightmare and fear began," I replied as I stood up. "I think I need a little break now. I need to use the restroom."

When I returned, I asked Sgt. Long if he wanted another drink, but he declined. "So, are you ready to hear more, Chris?" I asked.

"Whenever you're ready," he replied.

Chapter Three – The Nightmare Begins

"Okay, now where did I leave off? Oh yes, I was about to tell you the first night of terror. The same day my mother shared with me that Paul was not my real dad was the first night Paul was going to show me how special our relationship was going to be. It was late at night. I know this because all the lights were out in the house. My brother was sleeping in the room next to me and I was dreaming.

Paul entered my room and closed the door behind him. He sat on my bed next to me and then was lying beside me. He whispered softly in my ear while caressing my hair, words I will never, ever forget. He began to share again with me that we were about to have a wonderful relationship unlike any other parent and child could ever have. Of course, he mentioned again how expensive and time-consuming it was to adopt a child. At that point, he started to rub his hand against my belly and then slowly up my nightshirt to my chest. I felt his breath against my ear and then on my cheek. He kissed my lips hard and long. I could feel his tongue on my lips, and I remember thinking how weird that felt. He just kept telling me over and over again how special I was and how we were going to have a special relationship, but it was also very important that no one ever find out about this because my friends would be jealous and others would not understand.

I was scared of course and agreed that I would not tell anyone. It was then he got up and pulled my shirt down, kissed me softly, and told me he loved me before opening the bedroom door and leaving. He left the door open just the way it was, and I watched as he looked in on my brother who was sleeping. I knew that they must not have had a special relationship because he just walked in and then walked right back out of the room. I watched him walk by my door and head downstairs. I must have laid in bed for a long time before falling asleep because I remember crying so much and so long that my pillow case was so wet that I needed to flip it over to the dry side. Paul still had not come back upstairs by the time I fell asleep.

"The next morning was rather strange for me. Part of me wanted to think that all of this must have been a bad dream, but I knew it had happened. How should I handle this? Should I do things as normal? I guess so.

When I went down-stairs, my mother was already in the kitchen preparing a wonderful breakfast, which we ate together as a family. My mother, father, and little brother all sat in the usual places, and we carried on like any other normal family. After getting ready to start the day, I went about my usual routine of playing outside with my friends. Playing with them almost put the night before out of my mind. Then it was time to come in for the night. My mother said it was time to get cleaned up and get ready for dinner. It must have been a weekend because Paul was home all day, and he was working on his work car. It was an old Volkswagen but it worked.

"We ate dinner as a family and then did the usual family evening stuff, whether it was watching T.V. or playing a game. When it was time to go to bed, my mother usually tucked my brother and me in at night. He usually went to bed about an hour before me. Once I was in bed, my mother and father at separate times would both say goodnight to me.

"The very next night following Paul's first visit to my room, when the house was dark and I was sleeping, Paul entered my room and shut the door behind him. This time he picked me up from my bed and gently put me on the floor by the foot of my bed. He had a warm washcloth with him. He was hovering over me and whispered again to me how much he loved me and how special our relationship was, even more-so now. He took my pajama bottoms off and lightly caressed the warm washcloth over my vaginal area. He then softly kissed the same area. He then put his hands on my knees and spread my legs apart. At that moment I realized he did not have any clothes on. He got down on his stomach

12

with his head between my legs. He then performed oral sex on me for what seemed like forever. He then sat back up and pulled me by the hips until my bottom half was up against his bottom half. I was flat on my back, and he was kneeling down over me. He gently told me that it was going to hurt a little and then entered his penis into my vagina. The pain was more than I could handle. The tears fell from my eyes so fast and hard that my eyes were burning and my ears were filling with tears. I held onto the gold shag carpet with all my might and just hoped the pain would stop but more importantly that he would leave me alone.

"When he was done, he used the cloth on me again, put my clothes back on me, and dressed himself. He then picked me up and put me back in bed. He leaned over me and reminded me that it was important that this remain a secret between us, but this time he told me it would be terrible if my mother ever found out about it. I had no idea what that meant, but it scared me. Again he left the room, checked on my brother, and then went downstairs. I cried the whole night. I remember touching myself over my pajamas. The throbbing pain and the strange feeling were horrible. I kept thinking I wasn't sure if this special relationship was at all what I wanted. Maybe having the relationship my friends had with their fathers was special enough.

"Again, the next day was the normal routine kind of day. I think back now and wonder how he could have enjoyed this. I was a little kid. My body was that of a child. I had not developed breasts, and the vaginal area was small-- what I considered to be fragile.

"You have to understand, that from outward appearances, we had the perfect little family. Paul was a wonderful provider; we lived in a beautiful townhouse in a small New England town. We were considered to be upper-middle class. My mother was a wonderful homemaker; she was extremely involved in my school. I went to Sunday school each week. We even went on family vacations like normal families. We would have Sunday picnics or cookouts with relatives either from my mother's side of the family or from Paul's side. It was great; we had a lot of fun with these people. I remember one time; we had a huge cookout with all the family including aunts, uncles, cousins, and family friends. We played games, ate lots of food, and just had a blast. We had wonderful Christmases and terrific birthday parties. My mother always made the holidays extra special, like something out of a storybook. I even remember one birthday when my mother made me a Barbie Doll cake. It was purple and white, and it was the prettiest thing I had ever seen. It's the kind of cake that you see in the store. All of our birthdays were like that; we always had a special cake. I cherish these memories so much. These were the times that I put the pain and fear in the back of my mind. I will be forever grateful for those wonderful memories.

"You know I said we took vacations as a family, well we did but thinking back Chris I can only recall two vacations where they were really vacations for me…meaning I was left alone. One was a cruise we took to the Bahamas; I was left alone by this monster I guess because we were all in the same cabin. The other was when we went to Disney World after we moved to Florida, again probably because we were all together in the same room. But when it came to vacations that we were visiting family in other states, Paul would make his nightly visits to see me, and one time Paul and I went camping with a neighbor who was a scout leader, we went along with them on an overnight, I was alone with Paul all night in a tent, and as you could only imagine that was a horrible night for me…one I will never forget. It's sad that with all the vacations we took as a family all of them are over taken with horrible memories when in reality some of them really were wonderful vacations, or could have been. One I will always remember was when we rented a house on a lake, it was great, my brother and I spent a lot of time swimming in the lake and fishing. We had a huge clam boil with friends and family we invited to join us…but as I said all these memories are tarnished by the terror Paul caused over and over.

14

"I know this is going to sound terrible, but I remember one time while spending the night at my best-friends house we were watching television and the evening news was on, they were talking about a terrible truck accident that was actually not far from my house. Since my father was a truck driver and it was a truck from the same company as his I thought it might be him. The lady on the news said it appeared the driver was killed on impact. I told my friends mother I knew it was my father could we please drive by the accident so I could see for myself? This lady was a bit on the crazy side and agreed to take me. I even told her not to call my mother and upset her, I wanted to first check it out myself and see if it was his truck. We drove by the accident and I remember my friend holding my hand and telling me it was going to be okay. When we passed the truck I noticed a sticker of a cartoon character on the door of the truck…I started to cry. Of course my friend and her mother freaked out thinking it was Paul…but it was not. My friends mother stated that I must be crying because I was relieved it wasn't my father…I remember choking on that thought and agreeing with her. Of course that night I felt bad that I was thinking these horrible thoughts and thought of the poor family that this man belonged too.

"Anyone looking into our house would never believe that such terrible things could be happening here. The molestation was kept a secret because I acted as the perfect little daughter, and Paul appeared to be the perfect father. My mother never would have suspected anything, even if she woke up and discovered Paul wasn't beside her. He complained of back trouble and insomnia a lot, so it wasn't odd for Paul to get up and 'sleep on the couch' when his back 'hurt'. You know I often wonder what would have happened if I wasn't the "perfect" little daughter, what if I yelled out or told someone…but my fears for my brother and mother always took over. I wasn't sure what Paul meant when he would whisper those little threats into my ear. But I have to wonder what if I said something back then…maybe these poor children in Paul's neighborhood wouldn't have been tormented the way they have, I only hope they will not be scarred forever by him. I am so sorry this happened to them, I didn't know that Paul would do this to "strangers" I just thought it was a sickness he had with me. Wow, time to take a deep breath here.

"Elaine, we can take a break if you want here?" asked Chris.

"Oh no I will be fine let's just keep going for now, so...then the day came that my mother decided to take a part-time job at a hotel in registration. She worked sporadic nights and weekends, but it sure felt like a lot more. Now Paul was the only adult in the house, so the chances of getting caught were very slim.

"Paul was pretty brave about the sex. I remember clearly one weekend morning, when my mother was at work; my brother and I had slept in. When we got up, Paul decided it was still too early to go downstairs, so he had us come into bed with him. Paul was under the covers naked, and had my brother on top of the covers, playing with some small toys from his toy box. Paul was making jokes and laughing, but he had me under the covers sitting on top of him. He wanted to play a 'bouncing' game with me. Right in front of my brother, this man had his penis inside of me. At the same time, he was trying to tickle my side so I would laugh instead of cry like I wanted to.

"I was molested at least three times a week from age seven to approximately ten years of age," I said with a big exhale of air.

"Then it stopped?" asked Long.

"Oh, no. I thought it was going to stop, but there was more to come." I replied. "It was only the beginning."

Chapter Four – Becoming a Woman

"Now I am about ten years old and I started my period. I was now a woman. Wow! From what my mother told me, I could now have a baby. Not that I wanted one. It was just weird to know that once you get your period, you can have babies. It was about a year or so earlier when my mother shared with me the facts of life. She started her period extremely early in life, so she wanted to be sure I was prepared and knew what to expect. This was something she knew nothing about when she became a woman. She was scared and thought she was dying or something.

"Now that I was a woman, I thought Paul would finally have to leave me alone. After all, he didn't want to get me pregnant. I remember wearing Kotex pads before I even started my period because I thought it was pretty cool. I wore it to bed one night, and Paul came into my room, felt the pad, and left. It immediately rang in my head that if I wore a pad all the time, Paul would not be able to do all these horrible things to me. Then I noticed that he would go into my brother's room. My mind started going crazy. Was he doing something to my little brother? I have always been very protective of him, and the thought of someone hurting him was very upsetting to me. I remember feeling scared when he went into my brother's room after feeling the pad, so I jumped out of bed and went into the bathroom. I made a lot of noise, so much so that Paul came right out of the room, and went downstairs. I then went into my brother's room to check on him, and he looked peaceful as he slept.

"It was then I knew that I could not do something as stupid as wearing pads when I didn't even have my period. I knew what Paul was doing to me was wrong and scary, but no one was going to hurt my brother if I could help it.

"So, when I finally started my period for real, I was excited. Paul was going to have no choice but to stop. But I was wrong. Paul shared with me the night I really had my period that I was not to worry. Our relationship was going to become even more special now. Now that I was a woman, things were going to feel even better to me. I also never had to worry about getting pregnant either because he had a vasectomy after my brother was born.

"He also wanted to show me something else about him. He said that he always felt ugly when he looked at himself naked, but now that we had such a special relationship, he felt he was special, too. He then showed me his penis; he showed me that he was never circumcised. Being like this meant he was special. He had me touch it and push the skin back; he even made it like a game. When the skin was pushed back, he'd make a 'pop' noise and laugh and say something like 'there it is' in a baby voice. It was then he asked me to kiss it goodnight. I refused, but then he pushed my head towards it and just told me to kiss it, so I did it real quick. He then kissed me real hard, shoving his tongue into my mouth until I felt myself gagging. He then lifted my shirt and starting licking my nipples. The next thing I knew, it was over. He put my shirt down, kissed my forehead, and left my room.

"After he left to go downstairs, I got up and went to the bathroom to brush my teeth. I then sat on the toilet to go to the bathroom. While my pants were down, I looked at my pad and just started to cry. I really thought that once I really needed one of these, I would not be treated like this anymore. My mind was just reeling faster and faster. When will this stop? Nothing is going to prevent it, not even becoming a woman."

"I am so sorry Elaine, but you are doing a great job telling me everything," said Sgt. Long.

"I think I need a little break," I replied. I got up, went into the bathroom, and splashed some water on my face. When I returned, I once again asked Sgt. Long if he wanted anything to drink. This time he agreed to have a Coke. I then sat down and prepared to share with him our move to Florida.

Chapter Five – The Move to Florida

"It was extremely exciting to find out that we were moving to Florida. Of course, when I thought of Florida, I thought of Mickey Mouse and the beaches. It was great. The reason we were moving was because my uncle and Paul were going to start a trucking company in Florida. Paul and my uncle went to Florida ahead of us to research the business and look for a place to live. When Paul returned, he told us that he had found us a beautiful home in a beautiful neighborhood.

"I couldn't wait to go to school to tell everyone we were moving. The day before we left, my class gave me a great going away party. They gave me suntan lotion, sunglasses, a little portable fan, and all kinds of neat other stuff. My teacher made cupcakes, and we had punch and just played music and cool games. It was the best. I felt so lucky.

"I remember clearly the day we arrived in the Sunshine State. Our furniture hadn't arrived yet since we arrived ahead of the movers. We stayed on the beach for a few days while we waited. It was great. The hotel was huge and the beach was right behind it. I played with my brother in the sand; we ate out at night and drove around to become familiar with the area. It was so much fun, more like a vacation.

"When Paul took us to the house, we were all so excited. It was only a two-bedroom house, but it had beautiful wooden floors with a large back yard with tangerine trees. It was going to be great. I was very happy about the sleeping arrangements because my brother and I were going to share a room. I know most kids would have been freaking out to find out they had to share a room with their little brother, but I thought it was wonderful. I figured Paul would not be able to do all those horrible things to me with my brother right next to me. It also meant that I could keep a closer watch on my brother. I knew now that we were safe, which was a great feeling.

"I remember the day we moved into that house. It was October 30, 1978. I was eleven years old. My mother signed my brother and me up for school. I was a little concerned about starting a new school. It was pretty far from home, and back then they were still segregating black and white populations. That was all new to me.

"I was sent to a school that required almost a forty-minute bus ride each day. After starting at the school, I really learned to like it. I made a lot of great friends, and it proved to be pretty much like any other school except that I was not used to having so many black people in class. That scared me a little, since where I came from; I had never really seen a black person before. I knew one black person up north named Ramona, and I really never considered her to be black, but I'm not really sure why. But this was definitely a learning experience. My biggest concern for now was what I was going to be for Halloween the next night.

"Being new in the neighborhood, we weren't sure how many kids were around there. My mother bought my brother a pirate mask, and she put him in shorts and an old shirt. I wore some old clothes of my mother's and dressed as Mrs. Roper from *Three's Company*. Paul took us out trick or treating to a few of the homes in the area. It was funny because when my brother and I went to the door, people thought I was his mother, so they would want to give him candy. I had to explain to almost everyone that I was dressed up in a costume, that I was not his mother. It was a great laugh when I got home.

"My brother and I went through all the candy and put it into piles, one for the candy my mom liked, one for Paul, and, of course, our favorites. We then traded off candy. It was a great night. I was sure that the rest of the evening would be just as wonderful. I would get to sleep all the way through the night, and no one would come in and hurt me. Of course, though, I was wrong. I couldn't believe it. My brother was in the bed next to me, and Paul was crawling into my bed. He performed oral sex on me as he always did and then had sex with me until he'd had enough. He kissed

20

me hard, and then everything was returned back to the way it was before he entered my room. After he left the room, I rolled over and stared at my brother. I cried silent tears until I drifted off to sleep.

"This continued as usual until one night, while Paul was under my covers performing oral sex on me, a rustling sound came from my brother's bed. He wasn't waking up but was just rolling over and kicking his covers off of him. It scared Paul so much that he didn't move for a while and then decided that maybe we should move somewhere else in the house. But for now, he just got up and left the room.

"The next night, he came into my room and woke me up. He then held my hand and walked me into the family room. We walked through the living room into a family room. It had a little step down and French doors, which had off-white curtains hanging from them. He closed those doors and put me on the floor. The floor was hard. It had an ugly white and green colored shag carpet, but there was no padding underneath. He then removed my underpants and lifted my top. His pants were already off. He performed oral sex on me and then proceeded with intercourse after that. Once he was done, he put my clothes back on and walked me back to my bed. He tucked me in and then kissed me with an open mouth. His tongue was so far into my mouth I felt I couldn't breathe.

"This activity took place on a regular basis, but now it was about to take a little more of a twist. I got used to the idea that I could just lie there and not move while he did whatever he wanted to me. One time he had me in his bedroom. I'm not sure where my mother was. If I remember correctly, she was at the grocery store or running errands. Paul had me lay on his bed and all my clothes were taken off and as usual all his clothes were off. He then slid me to the edge of the bed while he was standing beside the bed. He had me roll onto my side where he then grabbed me by my hair. He explained that it was time for me to 're-pay' him for the wonderful oral sex he performed on me. It was then he took his penis and shoved it into my mouth. While the tears started rolling from my eyes and I felt myself gagging, he just told me to suck on it and keep moving my head back and forth, but more importantly not to stop. I remember trying to stop, but his fingers were wrapped around my hair, and he just kept shoving my head back and forth. I felt him shake hard and he moaned terribly. He kept telling me he was almost 'there' just as he said that, he pulled himself from my mouth and shoved his penis into my vagina. He pumped against me so hard, the pain was unreal. He then lay on top of me for a long time just breathing heavy in my ear and caressing my hair. He then told me that was the best ever, and he was proud of me. He helped to put my clothes back on, and he went and took a shower. I just sat and waited for my mother to return with my brother. It seemed like they were gone forever, but when they returned, Paul met my mother at the door lovingly. And don't you know, Paul returned to my bed that night again for more. He wanted me to perform more oral sex on him, and again he had to shove himself into my mouth and do all the movements.

"While in this house, my mother's younger brother, Dan, came to live with us for awhile and then another brother, Bob, came to stay for awhile. Even though the both of them at separate times were staying with us that did not stop Paul from doing all those horrible things to me. As a matter of fact, Paul almost got caught one night. Paul had me on the floor in the family room and a Corvette pulled into the driveway; the car belonged to my uncle Bob. Paul quickly dressed me because I would not help him. Pulling me by the arm, he ran across the living room and put me into bed. Seconds later, the door opened and Paul acted as if he was coming out of the bathroom. I could hear a couple of words being exchanged by them, and then Paul went back to bed.

"I always loved that Corvette. I remember one night; my uncle took me out with a friend to dinner and a ride down the beach strip. It was an awesome night; we had lots of laughs and just a great time. My uncle took us to a wonderful restaurant for dinner and really treated us like ladies. He was so cool. I really loved having him around. When he was home, it was always a sure thing that laughs were going to happen.

"It was funny--one afternoon he was napping on the couch, no doubt recovering from a late night out on the town. While he was sleeping, I decided to paint his toe nails bright red. He never even knew it. As a matter of fact, when he woke up, he decided that he needed to go to the corner store for cigarettes. He put flip-flops on, hopped in his cool car, and off he went. The whole time my mother and I were laughing. When he returned home, I watched him get out of the car and I knew then he had seen his toes. After he chased me down and tickled me, he was laughing so hard. He told me while at the check out counter he looked down and saw his toes. I truly cherish those moments, because unfortunately I felt I had more bad times than good ones growing up. I loved any moment that I could just laugh and forget anything else." "So do you want to hear more, because trust me Chris, there is a lot more?" I asked.

"Wow, Elaine, I just don't know what to say. I am so sorry that these horrible things happened to you," replied Sgt. Long. "If you want to tell me more, that would be great. All the information I can get the better for our case."

Chapter Six – Time to Move into a Bigger House

"We had been in the area now for a while, and things were going good. My mother and Paul decided that it was time to move into a larger home. I was now entering into high school. This house was a lot larger and sad for me. My brother and I now had our own rooms. I really hated that. It was going to be a little harder to watch over my brother, and, of course, Paul was going to have it easier now, too, since he didn't have to walk me through the house to molest me.

"Being in high school now, I really started to take interest in boys. I was in a typing class and met a guy who was just a friend. He wasn't the type of guy a girl would want for a boyfriend, just a friend. Well, he invited me to the junior/senior prom. I was so excited to be invited. After all, I was a freshman and I was going to the prom with a junior. Even if he was just a friend, it was great.

"My mother promised to take me to a wonderful dress shop that carried the most beautiful dresses. There were so many to choose from, and they were all so beautiful. I ended up getting a pale purple one that was worn off the shoulders. My mother did my hair for me and it was incredible. She put it up with a lot of little curls hanging down. My date for the prom wore a burgundy colored tux and showed up with the most gorgeous car. It was candy apple red with white leather. It was probably from the mid '60's, and it was a convertible. He had beautiful flowers for me that I wore on my wrist. Paul took a lot of pictures of me and of the both of us near the car. Before I left though, Paul whispered in my ear that this guy, friend or not, was just going to try to get into my pants, and he told me not to let him. It was also then he offered his little words of wisdom that were mentioned to me several times through my life: 'stiff pricks have no conscience' Elaine, and don't forget it. I shook it off, walked back out to my date (friend), and we left for the prom. I had a wonderful time and wore a great smile the whole night.

What was even better was when we pulled into the driveway; I realized that Paul's words of wisdom were so wrong. I loved it!!!

"Summer was great; I did a lot of fun things with friends and really enjoyed Friday nights and Saturday nights because I would go to the local skating rink. The music was loud, the lights were dim, and the skating was awesome. I loved skating and at that time, roller dancing was big. Everyone did it.

"It was then I really found myself not being able to handle what Paul was doing to me. Paul would drop me off at the skating rink, and, once he was gone, I would hop in a car with some friends. We would head over to a local park where we would drink cheap wine and maybe smoke a little pot. Pain was a thing of the past while I was with my friends. Of course, I fooled around with a couple of them. Besides I didn't want to be labeled as a tease. It also made me feel like I was betraying Paul behind his back; I was no longer that innocent little girl he was raping night after night. I didn't care if Paul or for that matter my mother found out...I think deep down I wanted to get caught. There were times we would be in the park and believe it or not it was your department that would drive through and flash the bright lights on us and we would all run. Secretly though I wanted to get caught...I just didn't care, but it never happened. I don't know what would have happened if I was caught but I just wanted someone to take me away.

"You have to understand, when Paul picked me up at night, he would ask me about the whole night. At first I would just say it was great, and I did a lot of skating. But that never seemed to really satisfy him, so I started to give him bits and pieces of details about the night so he knew I was having sex with boys and drinking. He didn't care about the pot smoking because behind my mother's back he would smoke it. I know it really ticked him off because he would start to speed. It wasn't the type of anger a father would get if he found out his daughter was doing the things I was doing. It was the type of anger like I was cheating on him. It

25

was a long ride home, even though we really only lived about ten minutes away. Part of me was scared of his reaction and part of me was happy because I thought that maybe, just maybe, he would get it and back off. Part of me hoped we would get in a car wreck or pulled over...something but my luck was never that good.

"The relationship between my mother and Paul was changing; in the beginning, I couldn't put my finger on it. My mother was always so protective of my brother and me, so she hid things well. Soon though it was bigger than her, and hiding it was no longer going to be possible. Paul was becoming extremely physical towards her. Paul would go off on my mother for no apparent reason. I know that sounds crazy and people think, well, she had to do something to provoke him, but in this case she could just walk by him, and he would fly off the deep end and pick a fight with her. It was terrible. She always had to walk a fine line with him, and I'm sure she really didn't know why. In the beginning, I wasn't sure either, but then I started wondering if it was because of me. And before you say, 'Oh no, Elaine, it wasn't your fault,' you need to hear me out. Face it. I was getting older now and even though I was still very much afraid of Paul, I found myself just shutting off all emotions when he came into my room at night. It used to be I would just lie there and let him do whatever he wanted. Now I would put up a little fight. When he tried to remove my panties, I would roll on my side making it hard. If he spread my legs, I would then lock my knees together. He really had to 'work' where before I didn't move. Sometimes he would just get frustrated and leave. It was then that I realized the next day he would hit my mother or throw something at her for no reason. The next time when he came into my room, if I didn't fight him and I let him have his way, he was then sweet to my mother the next day. You also have to remember, he threatened me a lot with remarks on how horrible it would be if my mother ever found out. I didn't know what he meant. Was he talking physically or what? I put nothing past this man. So, again, he was winning and again my horrible nightmare continued."

26

"Elaine you are remarkable, I can't believe how well you have held yourself together with all the torment you went through as a child," commented Sgt. Long.

"You know, I guess I never realized it or looked at it that way. It was just a way of living for me, and they were cards I was dealt with so I had to survive," I replied.

Chapter Seven – On the Move Again

"A lot of things happened in the new house. More bad than good for me, but that shouldn't be any surprise to you. The move from the other house to the new one was not a long move; it allowed me to stay in the same high school, which was great for me. The house was beautiful; it had three bedrooms, large living room, dining room, family room, and most importantly a beautiful pool with a privacy fence. My brother and I were out in the pool all the time. We would have friends over all the time to swim; we had a lot of BBQs. I liked the layout of the house because my brother's room was right next to mine, and this way I could keep an eye on him at night.

"At the same time that I thought the house was wonderful; it was a very sad place for me. Of course, Paul would continue his nightly visits to my room, but the difference was now I had a waterbed. Of course, they aren't quiet, so once again; Paul was dragging me from my bed and putting me on the floor. But before doing that, he would perform oral sex on me in the bed, and then he would have me do the same to him. He would roll me on my side so my head was in front of him. Again, as always, he would have to hold me by my hair and motion by head back and forth because I was not going to help.

"I just couldn't understand what kind of joy he could have been getting. I wasn't showing him any affection. I would lie perfectly still. If he wanted my arm around him, he had to put it there. If he wanted my legs a certain way, he had to put them there. He would work up a sweat, and it wasn't because of hot, passionate sex.

"By this time, I was fifteen years old, and I fell in love with a boy from another town. We spent a lot of time together, and I really enjoyed it because I was with someone I truly cared about and more importantly wanted to be with. I remember approaching my mother in the pool one day, telling her that maybe I should go on the pill. Of course, my mother was sweet about it, but she discouraged it. She said that after all, I was still a virgin and I really needed to wait that I was a little young for sex. I agreed with her and then remember swimming off to the deep end thinking, 'Oh mom, if you only knew. I haven't been a virgin since I was seven years old.'

"Well, one thing led to another, and my relationship was building stronger and stronger. I ended up making love with him and thought for the first time in my life, 'this is really wonderful.' I had no idea that sex didn't have to feel ugly. I actually felt beautiful and truly loved.

"Of course, when I came home, Paul would be right there in my room that night and wanted to know what I did with him. 'You better not be sleeping with him or giving him any blowjobs,' he would remark. I would say 'no, of course not,' and he would call me an f---ing liar. Then he would wash me off with a warm cloth and have sex with me hard and mean.

"A few months went by and, even though Paul was being so mean to me at night after being with my new love, I didn't care. He wasn't going to stop me from being with him. I then found out I was pregnant. My boyfriend and I decided that we needed to keep it a secret until we could make arrangements at a local clinic. It was so hard to hide from my mother. She knew something was up because, when he would call, I would take it in another room. I appeared to be more distant than normal.

"Finally one morning, after finding a letter to my boyfriend that time was running out and we still did not have all the money together, my mother confronted me. She was wonderful; she was soft talking and very understanding. She said we would handle this together. I stayed home from school that day; she called Paul and told him what had happened and that she was taking me to the doctor that day. My mother never yelled or even seemed upset with me. We went together to the doctor, and then she took me home. Because of the layout of the house, she said it would be

29

easier if I stayed in her room for the day to rest. This way she could hear me if I needed something, and there was a private bathroom in there I could use. She helped me to change and fixed the bed up for me with lots of pillows and just sat with me, not really saying anything. She really didn't need to. I knew she loved me and that was all I needed then. I called my boyfriend and told him what had happened. He cried and was so ashamed and afraid to face my family. I told him to give me a few days and I would be in touch.

"When Paul returned home from work, he came into the bedroom never saying a word to me. He went into his closet, then into the bathroom looking at me but never saying a word. When he came out, he came up to me and I expected to get the same reaction as I got from my mother. After all, he loved me, right? Well, I got just the opposite. He said I was nothing but an f---ing baby killer and it serves me right. If I hadn't cheated on him, this would not have happened. Then he threw a little pillow at me and left the room. For a while, it was great having him mad at me for this because he stayed away from me. On the other hand, it made me nervous for my brother. I tried so hard to watch out for him. I only hope I was successful.

"After a month or so, Paul went right back to his normal routine and he was back to his sweet little self. My relationship with my boyfriend came to a sad end. It was a horrible thing for me, but I understood. It was hard for him to face my family.

"I started dating again, and, for a while, it just seemed like the same old thing, I didn't have feelings for those boys and I let them do whatever they wanted, just to get it over with. I remember one night in particular when this guy Greg and his friend showed up at the house to pick me up. We were going to a friend's house to hang out. Paul approached Greg and told him to have a great time with me and patted him on the back. He then leaned over to me and whispered in my ear not to have too much fun. Well, I went with Greg and his friend to my friend's house and one thing led to another and Greg and I had meaningless sex. My old feeling was back that I was to just go through the motions and give the guy what he wants whether I want to or not.

"That is not the only time I did this type of thing. One time while with a friend on the beach, we met two men, and I mean men. They had to be at least thirty-five years or better. I was about fifteen or sixteen years old, and they were fishing at a local pier. We started flirting with them, and the next thing I knew we were back in one of their condos on the beach. After smoking a joint with them, one of them led me into his bedroom. I again 'put out' for him and then walked out into the living room, and the other guy commented that he picked the wrong girl; he should have gone with the sure thing instead of the little tease he ended up with. I felt like such trash and dirt, but at the same time I just didn't care.

"Do you know what I mean? At that point in my life, I just didn't care about my self-respect or myself. Why should I? I had this man I called 'Dad' doing all these horrible things to me night after night. This was the person that should have been protecting me; instead the monster was already in the house with me. I just didn't value life or myself anymore, and I wasn't sure what to do about it. The thought of killing myself was never an option. I never thought about it because, even though I was feeling all this pain and going through all this terror, I could not imagine ever leaving my mother or brother. My mother has always been my best friend, and I love her very much and my brother is my 'baby' brother, I love him with all my heart. So, I continued to just carry on as usual and be the happy-go-lucky daughter and sister that I was day after day".

Chapter Eight – The Fear and Terror Carries On

"So, are you ready for more, Chris? It's funny. I know all these horrible things happened to me, but it's something that I have been able to block out and not that I can forget, but I have somehow been able to allow myself to stop feeling all the fear and terror that I lived day after day. That is, of course, until now. All the emotions are flowing again and once again so is the terror. When I close my eyes at night, I relive all this fear again. It's a feeling that I learned to close out of my daily thinking and now once again, it's hitting me right in the face, and deep down, I don't know if I am as strong as I used to be. That scares me.

"Another memory that will forever haunt me is when my mother and brother went away up north for a long weekend. I believe that I couldn't go because of school. So now, I was going to be alone with this man night after night while the rest of my family visited family. I dreaded the nights. I actually found myself coming home from school and napping a little before Paul got home, so I could handle the long night of no sleep. I knew that I had to keep one eye open because, with no one in the house, he would be able to roam free about the house at any time. And that is just what happened. The first night, which I believe was a Thursday, was a long one. Paul tried to do things to me while I was doing homework and then while watching T.V. My goodness, I couldn't even go into the bathroom without him at the door asking what I was doing and if he could help. Needless to say, I didn't sleep much that night at all. On Friday, I had a date with a guy I was pretty serious about. Paul seemed to like this guy but, of course, always asked me a lot of questions about our dates.

"I went on my date and, of course, Paul was waiting up for me, wanting to know what we did on our date, whether we had sex, and, of course, the all-important question, whether I performed oral sex on him. I felt pretty much in charge knowing he couldn't hurt my mother or say horrible things to my brother if I stood up to him. So, I told him it was none of his damned business. He then pushed me up against the wall and told me to never talk to him like that. I was not to be disrespectful to someone who loves me the way he does. It scared me. I had felt so strong and, in an instant, he brought me back to feeling powerless and scared. He then told me to go take a shower because he was not going to sleep with me after betraying him by f---ing someone else.

"I went into the bathroom and sat there for a moment on the edge of the tub feeling so sick and wondering what was going to happen next. I then got into the shower and the next thing I knew, Paul was opening the shower curtain. He was naked. He then got in with me and said he was going to wash me clean. I just stood there with my face in water so he couldn't see the tears. I tried to focus on the night I'd just had with Allen. I truly loved this man and knew that someday we would probably be husband and wife. He then shut the water off, and once again, I was back with him. He then dried me off with a towel and put powder on me. The smell of the powder is something I will never be able to get rid of. It wasn't the kind of powder you would put on a baby or something. It was a deodorant powder. To this day, the smell of it could make me sick. He then led me to his bedroom. He made me spend the night with him in my mother's bed. It wasn't bad enough that he was doing all these disgusting things to me on a regular basis, but now he wanted to play house and have me sleep with him the whole night in his bed.

"That was a night that my eyes never closed. I couldn't wait until morning; I was meeting Allen for breakfast and then going to the flea market. Of course, when the morning came, Paul once again wanted sex. I argued with him and told him that Allen was on the way, and I had to get ready. I also told him that I wasn't feeling very good. He acted like a little child that morning. While I was trying to get ready, he was following me around. He would touch me and try to kiss me. By nine o'clock, I was out the door, and I didn't come back until late that night. It was only one day away before my mother and brother would be back, and I couldn't wait. But before that would happen I would have another evening and a morning with Paul.

"When I entered my room that night, I figured Paul was already sleeping because I didn't see him. He was in bed all right; he was in my bed, waiting for me. He thought it might be nice to sleep the whole night in my bed for a change. So, after another evening of torture, he went to sleep, or I should say he tried to sleep. I purposely tossed and turned on the waterbed to make it move. I did this so much that he finally got up and went back to his room. I was finally able to close my eyes and get a little sleep.

"The next morning, Paul was in my room bright and early and told me to get changed into my swimsuit because we were going to have a swim before breakfast. I really didn't want to swim, especially with him. But I agreed and met him out at the pool. When I went outside, he was already in the pool down by the deep end. He was leaning over a raft. He told me to jump in--the water was great. I got in but stayed down in the shallow end. He kept calling me to come down to the deep end. I refused and he just kept begging. Finally, he came down towards me with the raft in tow. When he got closer, I realized he was naked. He then pulled the straps from my suit and told me to lie on the raft. I told him that there was no way in hell I was getting out of this pool and laying on a raft naked. He just kept telling me it was okay, that no one could see, and even if they did, they would love to see me. They would be jealous that they couldn't have me the way he could. I still refused. He began swimming under water, trying to put his head between my legs. He would blow bubbles and stick his fingers inside of me. I told him I'd had enough of the water and was going in.

"I grabbed a towel and went inside. He followed me and, before I could go to my bedroom, he stopped me by grabbing me hard by the arm. He then told me we were going to have one last hour of delight before the return of the rest of the family. He led me by the hand to the dining room where he had me lay on the table with my bottom half where he used to sit for dinner. He then told me that he was going to 'eat' breakfast. He performed oral sex on me for a very long time and then had hard sex with me; he even bit me on the nipple. Oh, did I mention that I was not to call him 'dad' that weekend? He wanted me to call him 'Paul.' I then got up and went into the bathroom to get ready for my mother and brother's return. I couldn't wait. I really missed them and needed them back.

"We went to the airport, and on the way, Paul kept thanking me for a wonderful weekend. What did this guy see; I didn't do a thing to make him think for one minute I was enjoying this. I lay perfectly still and never, and I mean never, showed any type of emotion. This man is truly sick, and I would never get away from him as long as I lived home. But I was still in school and only about sixteen or seventeen years old.

"We finally arrived at the airport and happily my mother and brother were back with us, and to me I knew that the daytime torture was at an end for now."

Chapter Nine – The Scent of Evil I Will Never Forget

"Wow, Chris, I'm sure this is more than what you bargained for isn't it?" I asked.

"Well, to tell you the truth, Elaine, I am overwhelmed. I am so sorry that you went through this," replied Chris.

"You know, Chris, it's strange. I guess I just didn't know any different when I was younger because this was something I went through night after night. Then, as I got older, the fear was more than I could handle, so I really never felt sorry for myself. It's getting late, so let me share with you some of the final days at home."

I took a deep breath; my dog was sleeping on my lap. I just continued to pet him softly. It's amazing how calming dogs can be when you are dealing with such a stressful matter.

"I told you a little about Allen. Well, I knew this was the man that would forever be in my life. Our dating was getting very serious. He lived in a small apartment not too far from me. I would go out with him on special dates, and he treated me like I was the only woman in the world. We would go to dinner, he would take me to the beach at night with a bottle of champagne or wine, and we would dance under the stars with the cool, white sand under our feet. He told me he loved me and he really meant it. It was such a great feeling to have a person who really loved me and didn't want to hurt me.

"Paul was very jealous of this. He would tell me over and over again how Allen wasn't any good for me and that in the end, he would only hurt me. Only he (Paul) was right for me, and someday I would realize that.

"I would see Allen every chance I had. I felt so good when I was with him. I even went with him up north at Christmas one year to meet his family and friends. It was great to see where he grew up. More importantly, it was nice to be able to sleep at night and not have a fear or care in the world. Or almost anyway. I still worried about my brother and wondered if he was safe at night. Of course, there was no way to check. I certainly couldn't ask him, and Lord knows I wasn't going to confront Paul about it.

"More and more, Paul would visit me at night and more and more I was beginning to hate him. He would always come into my room freshly showered and clean and wearing cologne that to this day makes me sick to smell. I can smell it right now while I'm talking to you. I would smell the cologne on clothes and myself until I washed it off, but I swear the smell would stay with me day after day.

"Time was passing and the usual behavior was continuing except now Paul wanted me to spend more time with Allen. There was a time when Paul and my mother were going out (to separate places) and Allen was coming over. We were going to swim and just hang out. Paul suggested to me that I swim with Allen naked in the pool and maybe even have a little sex with him. He had such an evil laugh when he was suggesting this to me. I made no comment to his remark, but as he was leaving and Allen was coming in, they said their hellos and Paul would look over to me and wink and tell me to have a great swim. I wanted to vomit right then and there.

"Of course, I did not swim naked or have sex with Allen, first of all because our relationship was more special than that, and secondly, I had learned never to trust Paul's motives. Sure enough, I was right. Paul had come back early and decided to peek over the fence to hopefully catch us doing something. Allen did not see him and, of course, did not know what Paul had suggested. After a couple of minutes, Paul came in through the porch like nothing ever happened. He made small talk with us, left the pool area, and went inside. That night, Paul wanted to know why I disappointed him. He said he was looking forward to comparing himself with Allen, and I let him down. Under my breath I said that there was no comparison. Paul heard me, shoved me against the wall and asked what I'd said. I said I hadn't said anything.

"With all of this going on, we moved again. My mother always said the next new house was the move from hell. I later said it was the move that saved my life.

"I was spending a lot more time with Allen. We were talking about someday moving in together and even getting married. I would go to his place in the evenings; we would cook together, watch movies, and make love. One night we were in bed, and we kept hearing noises outside. Allen kept looking around out the windows but couldn't see anything. I went into the bathroom and part of me knew it was Paul but wasn't positive. Then I looked out the bathroom window, and I could see Paul sneaking around the side of the apartment towards the front. I went back to bed with Allen and told him it was probably a cat or kids. That seemed to satisfy him, and we went back to making love.

"When I got home that night, Paul was outside. We had a boat, and we usually kept it parked in the driveway. It was a fun boat. We would water ski and fish. We even went camping one time on an island, and Allen and I got to sleep on the boat (in separate beds) while my family slept on the island. Anyway, Paul was sitting in the boat with a drink. He told me he wanted to talk to me and to come up into the boat. I hesitated but went up into the boat. Paul had a towel on his lap. He asked me how my evening was. He started telling me how nice the sheets were on Allen's bed. He asked what it was like to have sex on black satin sheets. He mentioned the music playing and even the candles that were burning. I told him he was sick for watching me at Allen's that way. He grabbed my arm and told me to never say that again. He said I was sick and a slut for doing the things I was doing. He then removed the towel from the front of him and he was naked. He told me to get on my knees and do to him what I had done to Allen. I performed the oral sex on him but cried the whole time. I never wanted to vomit more than at that moment.

"I got up off my knees and off the boat. I went straight into the bathroom and brushed my teeth until my gums bled. I felt myself wanting to vomit, so I sat on the side of the tub for a while. I then went to my room and locked the door. Once again my night ended in fear."

Chapter Ten - The Break-Up

"As I said earlier, the move into this house was the best thing ever. My mother again said that it was the house from hell.

"I graduated from high school and had a great graduation dinner with family. It was something I was very proud of; Allen was so happy for me and so proud. My family all attended the graduation, and it was nice to have something positive to celebrate, even if it was just for an evening.

"Things between my mother and Paul were extremely tense. Paul had been extremely violent toward my mother. As I said before, I really believe it was because of me. Things were going great between Allen and me, and Paul hated that. Taking it out on my mother was something that Paul knew would affect me, and it did. I knew that I had to do whatever Paul wanted--that is until one day when I 'snapped.'

"My mother and I had been out shopping for the day. When we came back, Paul was on the couch watching television. He asked my mother where his beer was. She asked him what he was talking about. He went into a rage and said he wanted to know where his f---ing beer was. She told him she didn't buy any that we were clothes shopping, and we did not go to the grocery. He got up and followed my mother into the kitchen. He then threw a knife at her. Fortunately it missed. He then slammed her over and over and against the wall. I just snapped and I went after him. I slammed his head over and over and over again into the wall. I asked him how he liked it. I remember doing this to him until he cried and begged me to stop. I finally stopped and walked out the front door, I took off on foot to my uncle's house.

"Allen and my brother were out biking. When they returned, my mother sent Allen out to look for me. He knew that I was more than likely at my uncle's since he didn't live far away. He picked me up and brought me back to my house. He then kissed me softly and told me to go back inside to talk with my mother. I did and he drove away. Once inside, my brother, mother, and Paul were all sitting the living room. My mother said we all needed to talk. She said that this cannot continue, and she and Paul needed to get a divorce. I will remember this as clear as if it happened yesterday. I remember that no one cried a single tear except for Paul. My brother had a look of relief, and I smiled right at Paul. He had such a look of disbelief. I believe that was the bravest thing my mother ever did. Standing up to Paul was always a risk, and she did it. I was so proud and happy for her. I really believed this was it, and my mother would see it through to the end, and she did just that.

"While packing for my brother and her to move, I packed as well, but to move in with Allen. It was great to see such happiness in my mother's face and, of course, my brother, too. Paul seemed to not believe that this was really happening. Each night my mother would pack more boxes plus prepare meals as usual. She even prepared food for Paul; she would leave it covered for him. I really believe that he thought this was a 'game.'

"Towards the end, Paul would come into my room but not to molest me. It was to tell me that he met someone new. He told me this woman was wonderful, and she was really there for him. I felt like he thought 'we' were breaking up. It was really rather gross.

"My mother and brother moved into a nice little apartment, and they both seemed to be so happy. As for me, I loved every minute of being with Allen. It was great to sleep and not have the fear in me that I had experienced for ten years.

For once in my life I was living without fear, and that was a wonderful feeling."

Chapter Eleven – Helping the Case against Paul

"Well, Chris, I hope this is enough to help your case."

"Elaine, it is more than enough. Of course, you know that we will need your help further. Just telling me about this is not enough. We need you. You are a victim, and your testimony is critical when it comes to putting Paul behind bars."

"Well, I just don't know if I can do this. I thought telling you would be enough, and you could do whatever you needed for your case."

"Elaine, you don't understand. Without you, there is no case. What you told me today could put him away for a very long time. I have some ideas on how you can better help with the case. Are you up for hearing that?"

"I guess so," I replied.

"Well, we do what is called a 'controlled phone call.' It is legal. We use them all the time. Basically, in a controlled area, whether it is here or at the police station, you would call Paul and get him to talk about the past and we will tape it."

"You mean I would have to actually call him and talk to him about this?"

"Yes, but let's not worry about it right now. I want to talk with my superior first and see what he suggests. I just think this would be a great step towards getting this child molester behind bars. Of course, Elaine, you know you're going to have to tell your mother, right?"

"I haven't thought of that. I guess I am going to have to think of a way to tell her. This is going to kill her, you know. I tell my mother everything. This is the first time I have ever kept something so horrible from her."

"Elaine, if you would like, I could plan on being here with you when you tell her. It might be easier for the both of you."

"No, Chris, I have to do this myself. Just please do not call me here at home, or my mother, until I call you, I want to tell her everything. Is that okay with you?"

"Of course it is. Just call me after you speak with your mother." He then handed me a red booklet that was for victims. He told me that it would answer a lot of questions I may have, and it also had a phone number on it to a victim advocate.

We said our good-byes, and I tried to regain myself before my son got home. I also knew that I had a lot of telephone messages from customers that had built up over the hours I was with Chris. I took my dog out for a well-deserved walk and then went back in to just check the messages. I was too worked up and upset to work, but I knew I had to at least see if any important calls had come in.

When my son came home from school, I had to try my hardest to act as if work was going as usual. I even sat in my office but mainly found myself just staring at the computer. Deep down I knew that I would have to work with Chris to get this man off the street. I knew that I did not want to do the controlled call here; the thought of talking to Paul in my home gave me a horrible feeling. First, of course, I had to tell my mother. My God, I never thought I was ever going to have to do this. I really believed that once I was away from him, everything would go away. I started feeling a lot of anger. I kept thinking, "Why couldn't Paul just keep his hands to himself? If he did, this secret would never have had to come out." Instead, he was leaving me no choice. Now a lot of innocent people were going to be hurt, and again it was all Paul's fault.

My mother came home and I asked about her day and she asked about mine. She shared things that had happened during her workday, and then she wanted to know what, if anything happened with me. The big question was always what kind of money making day I had. Of course, I knew I had done nothing, but I told her I had an average day. She then went about her usual business around the house, and I sat in my office staring at the computer. I shut down early; I told her I was having computer problems. We sat together in the living room and just made small talk. We then started dinner. I felt so sick that the thought of eating dinner seemed impossible. I felt as if nothing was going to go down my throat.

At dinner, I played with my food and just moved it around the plate. I probably only ate a couple of bites. I helped to clear the table and while clearing, I asked my mother if she would like to take a ride down by the beach. That was not unusual since we did that in the evenings as a way to just get out and unwind, especially since I work at home. Sometimes I just want to take a ride. My chest felt so tight I felt my blood pressure going up, and all I was doing was asking her if she wanted to go for a ride.

She agreed that it sounded like a nice idea. As always, we asked my son if he wanted to go for a ride and, as usual, he said he wanted to stay home and play video games. Since he was fourteen years old, he was certainly old enough to stay home alone. So, we finished up around the house and then got ready to go. My mother suggested that we take the dog with us; he loves to ride in the car. I thought it would be a great idea. She loved to hold him in the car, and maybe he would help her by being in her arms.

We headed out towards the beach. It was a beautiful mid-May night, the sky was clear, and there was no humidity in the air. We had the windows down and a light breeze was blowing. I kept thinking what a beautiful night it was, and I didn't want to ruin it. I felt my world was about to come crashing down. I took a deep breath, held the steering wheel tight, and said to myself, "Okay, here it goes."

"Guess who I spoke to today?"

My mother looked at me. "Who?"

"I spoke to Chris Long from the police department."

"What did he say? Did something come up with the case?" she asked.

Oh, God, here it goes, I thought. "Well, yes, I actually saw him today. I told him that I could help him with the case."

"What?"

"Yes, Mom, I'm sorry, but I had a lot of information that could help Chris with the case."

"Okay, Elaine."

I felt all choked up, and I could see my mother was, too. The good thing was I was driving, so I really didn't have to look at her--that is, of course, until she had me pull over.

"Chris had called me before I went away and then, when I returned, he wanted to meet with me. He felt strong that I would be able to help with the case when he found out that Paul had adopted me. He was right; I was able to tell him things starting from the age of about seven until seventeen years old. I am sorry I never told you. I was scared and afraid and then after the divorce, I thought that part of my life was over."

I then shared some of the conversation that Chris and I had and told her about the possibility that I may have to do a controlled call. She was full of questions of course and blame. I really tried to re-assure her that I knew she didn't know and if she did, she would have done something about it a long time ago. She needed to know that this man knew exactly what he was doing and he was good at it. In his eyes getting caught was never going to happen. As usual, my mother was extremely supportive and understanding. If possible, at that moment, I loved her more than ever. I so wished that I had told her earlier in life, but I didn't know what Paul would have done to her or my brother. I couldn't take that chance.

We drove a little more, and I had to run into the store to get my son something for lunch the next day. She wanted to wait in the car. I knew her mind had to be going crazy in the car, but I have to say that for the first time in my life, I felt a weight had been lifted from my shoulders. When I got back into the car, my mother just commented that she couldn't understand why she never saw anything. She kept saying, "Where was I, was I blind?"

"No, Mom, he was just sneaky and good at it. You can't blame yourself. Please don't blame yourself."

We drove back home and sat in the driveway for a while. We hugged each other and she said that she would stand beside me the whole way. We went into the house and prepared to settle in for the night. We both got changed into our nightclothes. I spent some time with my son, and then he turned in for the night. My mother and I watched some television and tried to not talk about it too much. We both went to bed pretty late that night. My mother had decided not to go to work the next day. She just wasn't feeling up to it.

That night proved to be worthless, as I was not able to sleep at all. I watched the clock and cried a lot. It was like my brain was replaying a movie over and over again but it wasn't a movie…it was my life. I replayed the whole conversation I had earlier with Chris. I still was asking over and over again why he couldn't have come up with an idea to solve this case without me. Of course I kept asking over and over why Paul just couldn't keep his filthy hands to himself. I thought about the day I found out this monster was not my real father, then I thought of my real father. My god he can't ever find out about this. He was very much part of my life now and when he came back into my life the first thing he asked me was if Paul was a good father to me and did he treat me well? Of course I told him that he was. He knew Paul was no longer in my life and never really asked why, maybe deep down he was afraid to know the truth. Needless to say my mind was reeling all night long. I was full of hate, sorrow, and fear.

When it was time to get up, I felt so horrible. I tried to act normal for my son and got him off to school as usual. After he left, my mother and I sat together and discussed me calling Chris. I went about my normal routine as much as I could and tried to get started on my work.

I called Chris and told him everything that had happened with my mother. He was glad to hear that everything went so well. I told him that if I really had to make the call, I would do it but only if it was really necessary. He told me he would be in touch and we hung up.

The rest of the day went rather quiet. Mom and I both were so exhausted that we really didn't have the energy to discuss it, nor did I want to. I knew that the road to come was going to be rough, and I was going to have to pull myself together and remain strong like I used to.

Chapter Twelve – The Controlled Phone Call

Chris called me and told me that he spoke with his superior and the state attorney's office. Both felt that a controlled call was critical to the case and if all went as planned; we could get enough to put him behind bars. Chris told me he would call me when we were going to attempt the call.

I tried to go back to work and concentrate on my job. Forgetting about Paul and everything that had happened proved to be almost impossible. Lucky for me, at that point, a call came in from a wonderful customer. This guy was always good for a great laugh, and again as always I got that laugh I needed so badly. For a while, I forgot all the terror that I knew was coming back into my life.

That evening, I still did not hear from Chris, not that I knew exactly when I was going to hear from him. I knew that when I did, it would mean that I had to go to the police station right then and there. I liked that idea because that meant to me that I would not have a lot of time to think about things. I would just go to the station and then do the call.

The next morning I was working, and the morning was business as usual. Then the phone rang about noon and it was Chris. He said that an officer in an unmarked car was patrolling Paul's neighborhood and noticed that he was home. Chris wanted me to come to the station right away. Of course, I hurried on this end and rushed to the station. On my way there, I called my mother on my cell phone and told her I was going to the station to make the call. She offered to meet me at the station and I told her that I would be fine. I promised to call her when I finished.

The ride there was quick, taking me about ten minutes to get there. I parked the car and sat for a minute before getting out. I looked at myself in the mirror and gave myself a well-needed pep talk. I told myself that I was strong and I was in control now and I COULD do this. I walked into the station and let the front desk officer know I was there to meet with Chris. I sat and waited for him to come and get me. The large door opened, and Chris was smiling as he waved me to come in. We walked the long hallways and took the elevator up to the office. We went into a long, narrow room that had a couple of telephones. We sat next to each other, and he then explained that I would use the phone in front of me to call Paul. If Paul had caller ID, it would come up as a business. Chris was going to wear a headset, so he could listen in on the call. A machine was going to tape us. He offered to turn the lights out if I wanted or we could sit back to back. I told him neither was necessary. We decided that we would use a pen and paper between us if Chris wanted me to ask questions or get something clarified.

Without hesitation Chris announced on the tape who I was, who he was, and the case number and date, May 29, 2002. I signed a form stating that I agreed to do a controlled phone call. By law, only one person in a telephone conversation has to give consent to be taped. At that moment, he dialed Paul's number and handed me the phone. I totally freaked out. I felt like I needed more time, but now the phone was being handed to me and I had no choice. Paul answered the phone on the third ring; the weird thing is he really didn't seem all that surprised to hear from me, but my heart was beating so fast I could hear it in my ears.

The following is the actual call that took place, as it was dictated for the police transcripts. Keep in mind that controlled calls don't always go smoothly and clearly. Some of the conversation may seem odd or off balance. That is because Paul kept jumping the conversation from one topic to another.

Paul: Hello?

Elaine: Paul?

Paul: Yes.

Elaine: Hi, it's Elaine. I need to talk to you. Do you have a minute?

Paul: Yes.

Elaine: Okay, this is pretty important for both you and for me. My mother and brother had a phone call and a couple of visits from an Officer Chris Long.

Paul: Yes.

Elaine: He said it was regarding some charges I guess that are pending or something against you from March or something.

Paul: March?

Elaine: I don't know, anyway just listen, okay?

Paul: Okay

Elaine: He came over; I guess he talked to both of them in detail asking a lot of questions about things, um, sexual questions that kind of stuff. I guess neither one of them were much help, I mean they answered questions the best they could, but really didn't have any knowledge of anything that was going on, so that was that with them. But, now this guy has been calling me, showing up at my work, showing up at my house....

Paul: Yeah.

Elaine: He has been leaving me all kinds of messages that he wants to talk to me and I have been avoiding this guy like the plague. I do not want to talk to this guy. This is something, you know, I haven't thought about this abuse, you know, that we went through.

Paul: Right.

Elaine: For a very, very long time.

Paul: Right.

Elaine: I didn't know if something happened when you were arrested that maybe you implied something or you told somebody something about the sexual abuse that I went through with you because this man is talking like he knows something.

Paul: Well, no. First of all Elaine, I was falsely arrested. Okay, you got a minute?

Elaine: Yeah, I'm at work, but I am in my office with the door shut, and I just needed to call you today because I don't even want to go home. I know he's going to be waiting for me.

Paul: Okay, this here, what you and I went through, I will not deny, Elaine, okay?

Elaine: Okay.

Paul: Before I married Betty...

Elaine: Yes.

Paul: I told her. I could not go into details with her, but I did say that something happened between us. So she's known all along.

Elaine: Okay.

Paul: Okay, um, this thing I was falsely arrested for...

Elaine: Yes.

Paul: It's totally false. It never happened and I went through hell, my wife and I went through hell. We're $13,000 in the hole. We're getting new attorneys and what we're trying to do is put some stuff together for a lawsuit.

Elaine: Right.

Paul: Because this is all false.

Elaine: Right.

Paul: But it's hard to do that because you're involving kids and it's a tough job, as a matter of fact, I got to meet with the attorney again this week. The State Attorney dropped all the charges.

Elaine: Right.

Paul: Because they had brought the kids in under oath and all that stuff and the kids had changed their stories. This never happened; I'm telling you the truth. I wouldn't lie to you.

Your brother is upset with me; he called and left me some nasty messages on my voice mail.

Elaine: Well, he is very upset. You have to understand when somebody shows up at your door and you hear the words child molestation and sexual assault and all this kind of stuff. What do you expect?

Now here I am talking to my mother about the conversation she had with Long because he asked her to discuss things with me in case I might know something. I am lying to her telling her I have no idea what she or Long is talking about. This concerns me, you know, I don't want to get involved in any of this. You have to understand I have a child. I don't want my name dredged through anything; I don't want to do any court appearances. I just want to know what I should do or say when this guy shows up at my door, because you know he will catch up with me.

Paul: All right.

Elaine: You have to know Paul this cop acts like he knows something; he even talks about when we lived up north. He even mentioned some of my old friends. How does he know the kids I grew up with?

Paul: Maybe your brother mentioned them to him.

Elaine: No, he was a baby then; he wouldn't know any of my friends.

Paul: I don't know. You know I don't know if our phones are being listened to or whatever, but whatever happened between us, I will not deny. If I'm ever, you know brought up for it, I'm ready for it. I mean it's going to be hell, but I'm ready for it. I owe that much to you. Of course I'd rather it never go there, though.

Elaine: Well, I would rather not be dredged through anything either. I've moved on.

Paul: Right.

Elaine: You know I've been perfectly happy with the way things have been. I haven't thought about this and now I feel like I'm going through all this again.

Paul: Right.

Elaine: You know this is not something I am proud of; I don't go around and brag about it you know.

Paul: Right. I know. But if you don't want to get involved, say it never happened. You're the prime person, if you tell this guy to get off your case; it never happened he would have no choice. He can't do anything about it.

Elaine: Except for in the last message he told me that if I didn't want to cooperate with him, then he would just have me subpoenaed to come in.

Paul: Right, if you're subpoenaed to come in, I don't know how you handle that either.

Elaine: Me either.

Paul: You know, I don't know if you could say that hey this never happened and leave it there or what. You know, even under oath, it's up to you.

Elaine: Well that scares me.

Paul: Yeah.

Elaine: You know, I mean, I don't want to be caught in any lies and something happen to me because I lied.

Paul: Right. Here we thought we'd be over it and it keeps on going. We're going through hell too. You know, I know you went through hell through your life. But, Betty and I are going through hell. It's not fair to Betty. If you want to keep in contact with me and let me know what's going on, but you know, just, if you want to just say no, you know what I mean.

Elaine: Well at this point, like I said, I just want to go back to the way things were.

Paul: Right.

Elaine: You know, I've been very happy, things are going wonderful and now this is happening and it's just like I said, it's very upsetting and sickening to me.

Paul: It's gonna bring out a lot of dirt and all the...

Elaine: ...but you are sorry for what you did to me?

Paul: Yes I am. Yep, are you, is this being recorded here?

Elaine: No, I'm at work.

Paul: You're recording me here right?

Elaine: No, I am not. I am at work.

Paul: You're recording me, Elaine.

Elaine: No, I am not. I am at work. I am at my job.

Paul: Whatever happened, yes, I am sorry. Okay, whether you're recording me or not.

Elaine: If you want to call me back, you can call me here at work.

Paul: Right.

Elaine: I'll give you my direct line to my office.

Paul: Right. But I'm not saying what did happen on the phone, okay.

Elaine: That's fine.

Paul: Okay. I hope your not recording this.

Elaine: I am not recording you. Like I said, I just wanted to know what if anything you had said to people...

Paul: No, nothing.

Elaine: You have to know Long is just so adamant about getting in touch with me, that he knows something.

Paul: Right.

Elaine: That I was sexually molested by you I mean he just keeps, you know, I thought at first it was just a trick and he was trying to pull me in to question me.

Paul: Right.

Elaine: But he's just, little things that he says is leading me to believe that he knows something.

Paul: Okay. Well another thing you're calling it sexual molestation and I was trying to figure out the years it happened and...

Elaine: I don't know what to call it, what do you call it?

Paul: Well the years it happened...

Elaine: Yeah?

Paul: ...are you recording me or not?

Elaine: I'm not, but I don't know what to call this.

Paul: Okay.

Elaine: I haven't thought about this.

Paul: I'll be honest with you okay?

Elaine: What.

Paul: I was, um, affectionate to you, Um, in the years I was going through hell with something else and you showed me affection, you showed me warmth, you showed me things that I did not have with someone else and I kind of fell for that. Okay. That's being honest.

Elaine: So, it's my fault.

Paul: No, that's not your fault. I'm not saying it's your fault Elaine. I'm saying you as a person, you as an individual were...

Elaine: You were my father, what was I supposed to do, not be affectionate to my father?

Paul: Right, you were...

Elaine: I mean...I was seven or eight years old.

Paul: No, I wouldn't, okay, we won't do this on the phone.

Elaine: Whatever.

Paul: I have been trying to figure out when this occurred; I'm trying to pinpoint exactly where it happened too.

Elaine: I know exactly when it started.

Paul: Okay.

Elaine: I know exactly when it started.

Paul: Right.

Elaine: We were up north and I was around seven years old because it was right after my mother told me you adopted me.

Paul: Well, I don't remember that. I don't believe that.

Elaine: Whatever. It happened in the first house, second house and third house and then came to an end in the fourth house.

Paul: I agree it happened in the third house.

Elaine: Well I just wanted to see what if anything you had said when you were arrested for the other molestation charges. Like I said, I've been avoiding him.

Paul: He really has been talking to your brother?

Elaine: I know he talked to him at least once. And he talked to my mother a couple of times, but she doesn't know anything.

Paul: If you ever want to meet, I'll talk to you. I don't dare do it on the phone, because right now I've got this sick feeling that you might be recording me.

Elaine: Well, that's fine. I can understand your apprehension.

Paul: All of this is totally false. This is, you know, it's not something for me to tell you over the phone and that you believe me. It's kind of like two, two and a half year history here. These kids were our neighbors, their parents said, you can call our kids your grand kids and we took them and their parents out boating and this and that.

Elaine: Right.

Paul: Just one, for a matter of a few minutes all this happened and I'm still working on making copies, I've got police reports. I got all kinds of things I'm working on now because I'm working towards a lawsuit. The only thing is the attorneys are hesitant of this; because you're talking with these kids, which the one girl is only nine years old.

Elaine: Right

Paul: You gotta put her through videotaping under oath, and all kinds of stuff. Judges and lawyers are not too crazy about that.

Elaine: You have to understand where I'm coming from, that it's hard for me to believe this. You know, only…

Paul: Believe what?

Elaine: …that you didn't do anything to these little girls.

Paul: All Right, No, I, I…

Elaine: You know.

Paul:…understand that, but I did not. You know, I did not. Why would I lie to you about this? If I'm guilty of something, Elaine, it's always liking kids, always enjoying kids around. We'd be playing in the front, play in the back and out of a hundred visits there's probably a couple of times I'd give'em piggyback rides and this and that and one night here they're horsing around. They all ganged up on me and this is the night this happened. And uh, you know, I, I, know what you're saying. You know, it's hard for you to believe me.

Elaine: But how can horsing around, I mean, obviously something happened or these kids believed something happened, and you know what I mean.

Paul: Right.

Elaine: Well all of this abuse that I went through with you or whatever you want to call it, when I look at my child I say, okay, I can't do this, you know. I open the newspaper everyday and see so many people coming forward after being sexually molested, and I think that this is something I can't do. But now I am being put into this situation.

Paul: Right.

Elaine: And, you put me there, with this.

Paul: Well, uh, I don't know, why don't you call me again or something? I wish we could meet cause on the phone here, I don't know.

Elaine: I don't want to meet you in person. I mean, I understand your apprehension, okay, cause I would probably feel the same way, but I am not comfortable with meeting with you.

Paul: Yeah.

Elaine: I haven't even thought about you, you know.

Paul: Yeah.

Elaine: I've just moved on, and I have been very happy up until the last couple of weeks. Chris Long is just getting more persistent. And I know he's going to nail me one day. And I just don't know what I'm going to do.

Paul: Right. That's a shame. I mean, I don't blame you for not thinking about me. But I miss you. I think about you all the time. I even have a picture right here of you and your brother.

Elaine: Yeah. You know before you kept talking about impacting your life and my life. What you did to me has been a big impact on my whole life.

Paul: See I don't want to say the words, because I don't know if we're being recorded or whatever, but…

Elaine: Well, unless someone has come into my office and added a recorder, we are not being recorded.

Paul: Well what I'm saying is before I married Betty, because I knew that maybe someday I would be facing something and I thought this is the least I could do for her. Because this woman is something else. She's an angel that's turned my life around. So I told her, like I said, could not go into details but she knew what I was talking about.

Elaine: And what did she say?

Paul: She, uh, you know, it was hard for her, but she understood.

Elaine: She has a child, doesn't she?

Paul: Yeah, she has three of them.

Elaine: I mean I just can't imagine what she must have been thinking, knowing she's got kids that obviously you're going to be around and you don't think that's in the back of her mind all the time.

Paul: Yeah, so I did tell her certain things and you know. I don't know how many years it's been but it's been you know its everyday things. You, you lived a life that was tough because of that. I am also living a life that is tough because of it. I know because I live in fear that someday someone will knock on the door because you know why.

Elaine: Well all right like I said, I just wanted to contact you to see what if anything might have been said.

Paul: Elaine, I swear to God and you don't have to believe me, but I swear I am telling the truth. There was no molestation with these kids and that is why I am putting a lawsuit together. If I were partly wrong or whatever I'd say oh thank god I got off and I'm going to be good for the rest of my life. But it never happened.

Elaine: Well, what, I mean what were they actually accusing you of. I mean was it sexual abuse, sexual harassment, or what.

Paul: No, no the bottom line is they took two months for me to finally find out from the police report what they were actually talking about, because when the police knocked on my door at two o'clock in the morning, and got us out of bed. The asked me four simple questions then hauled me off to jail on a $50,000 bail. And it took me two damn months to finally figure out what the hell they were talking about. I was accused by this nine-year-old of putting my hands down the back of her pants between her underwear and her skin all the way down to the crouch area.

Elaine: Déjà vu.

Paul: It never happened. As far as you I call it more loving affection, not molestation. But whatever happens I'm going to wind up losing everything.

58

Elaine: What would have happened if I had said something when I was younger?

Paul: What would have happened?

Elaine: Yeah.

Paul: I don't know.

Elaine: I mean, would you have denied it then do you think?

Paul: Well see your saying younger and I'm, saying it didn't happen when you were younger. That's what I'm saying.

Elaine: Would you have denied it?

Paul: The molestation part? Yeah I would have denied it.

Elaine: I don't get it; in the beginning when you were talking you told me you were sorry.

Paul: I am sorry that what did happen between you and I, did happen between you and I. I am sorry I hurt you, but what I am saying is that from what I remember what happened between you and I was not molestation.

Elaine: Well, to me it is, because I just don't think of a father and daughter having sex as affection. Can you understand what I'm saying?

Paul: well, like I say it's probably being recorded and you got me now, so. You know, I wish we could meet some place.

Elaine: Well we can't.

Paul: If we could meet someplace personally, we can do it, but if you've recorded me, you probably have me.

Elaine: Well, if you want to believe that, that's fine. Okay, well I am at work so I am going to have to go soon. I just wanted to hear from you what if anything you may have said when you were arrested concerning me. That is why I called.

Paul: It's a shame you don't ever think about me, because I think about you all the time. I can still see you the first time I met you, riding in the back of your mom's car.

Elaine: Well, it's almost time for me to head home. I'm sure that Chris Long will be waiting for me either by my car or at my house. I am not looking forward to this.

Paul: It's entirely up to you Elaine. If you wanna just say no it never happened, leave me alone. And hopefully it stops there and if not, well, and then we got a rough time ahead of us, you know.

Elaine: Yeah I know.

Paul: Well, it's up to you if you want to call me again. It's up to you, you know, I wish you would once in a while. I know you want to forget me or everything else, but you know, here on this end, I don't forget you.

Elaine: Well.

Paul: You know.

Elaine: I'm trying to forget that whole part of my life and move on. I have a great relationship with my father and that's just the way I want it.

Paul: I was going to ask you about that is he around or what?

Elaine: Yes, he is very much in the picture.

Paul: Good, I'm happy for you.

Elaine: Well, someone is knocking on my door, so I need to get going. My door is locked and people are not used of that.

Paul: If you want to, you know, you don't owe me anything, but it you want to do me a favor, give me a call once in a while let me know what is going on with this, okay?

Elaine: Okay, bye.

End of the first controlled call.

After that was over, I sat with Chris. He told me how good I did, but I was shaking so bad from hearing Paul's voice, I felt as if I was going to be sick. Chris walked me to my car and told me again how good I did and that he would be in touch with me soon. When I left the parking lot, I called my mother as promised and told her everything. Overall, I told her I felt it went good, and, more importantly, I was glad it was over.

When I returned home, I walked my dog and tried to clear my head. Once inside, I went back to my daily work routine and tried my best to put the earlier event out on my mind. I finished my workday, and my mother came home. I was telling her again all the little things I remembered from the call that I didn't discuss with her over the phone. We played out together how we thought the call would go with the state attorney. We tried to imagine what the next step was going to be. We decided that was enough for the night, and for the rest of the evening we did not discuss Paul or the case. We watched movies and ate popcorn and tried to have a few good laughs. The evening ended up being like the great evenings we used to have before Paul came back into our lives.

Chapter Thirteen – Bad News

A few days had passed, and I was back to work as normal. I had not heard from Chris and my mother and I really hadn't talked about it either. Work was going good. Being in sales, it is important that I make the daily quota that is expected of me. I was once again doing that and it felt great. The end of the workday was winding down, and my phone rang. It was Chris. He sounded like someone who just lost his best friend.

"I've got some bad news. I turned the tape over to the state attorney's office, and when they went through the laws, it appears that the Statute of Limitations had run out for your case. It looks like we will not be able to prosecute Paul for what he did to you," Chris sadly remarked.

I felt as if my world had just come crashing down around me. "So you're telling me that I hurt my mother and brother and tortured myself by making that call for no reason?" I said as I started to cry.

"I am so sorry, Elaine. I find it hard to believe myself, but I am not giving up. I know there is something we can do; I just have to find it. I am going to the law library to look up the law myself. Please hang in there, and I will be in touch with you as soon as I find the information I need."

We said our good-byes and then hung up. I felt like something had died inside me. The tears were more than I could handle. I called my mother and told her what had happened. I was feeling such anger and sadness at the same time. Once again, Paul had ruined things in my life. Because of Paul I hurt my mother and brother. Again I was asking myself why Paul couldn't just keep his hands to himself. My mother took the news hard, too, but she was at work and had to keep it together.

"When she got home, though, we both cried together, and then she became more of the level-headed one. She said that I should listen to Chris, that it seems that he is not giving up so quickly, and neither should we. My mother always seemed able to get me to calm down and get a grip on myself. I found myself having a lot of crying moments, and that really upset me because again I felt as if Paul was in control over me. He always controlled my fears and tears. Now again, after all these years, he was doing it again. Chris had to come back with some good news. This could not have all been for nothing.

A few more days had passed, and we still heard nothing from Chris. My nerves were on edge, and I found myself taking it out on everybody. Then I got the call I was both waiting for and dreading at the same time. This time though, Chris sounded a lot happier.

"Good news. I went to the law library and then confirmed my findings with the state attorney and it looks like everything is a go. It appears that when the attorney was looking at the law from 1978, he needed to focus on when you moved to Florida since that is the time frame we are prosecuting for. The wording of the law stating the age of the child was tricky. One little word was being mis-read and that is why the attorney's office thought we were past the time limit. We can prosecute Paul for October through the first part of January before your twelfth birthday. It is a small window of opportunity, but we can do it, Elaine." Chris said with a lot of enthusiasm in his voice. "We have a lot of work ahead of us, but we feel that we are on the right track. We're going to meet with the state attorney to see where we stand. I'll be in touch."

I let him know how grateful I was and we hung up. I called my mother and told her the whole thing. She was as happy as I was. I didn't do this for nothing after all.

On June 10, 2002, Chris, my mother, and I went to the State Attorney's office. My mother and I drove together and arrived before Chris. The attorney decided to meet with me first. I left my mother in the lobby where she waited to meet Chris. I was with the attorney for approximately ten minutes and I felt extremely discouraged. I felt as if I was wasting this man's time and, most importantly, I felt he didn't believe me.

I walked out of the office, and both my mother and Chris seemed very surprised to see that I was through talking to him. He didn't even want to talk to my mother. Chris and I talked for a brief moment before he was called into the office. My mother and I walked the long hallway, and I felt the tears building in my eyes.

"This man doesn't care. He asked questions like I was the bad guy. We will never have a case because this guy just doesn't care," I said to my mother as we walked to the car.

"Elaine...maybe that's just his approach. He has to be cautious that is his job. Just wait and see what Chris has to say," she replied. She was right, of course, but the feeling I had when I was in that office was not the same warm feeling I had with Chris. Chris believed and trusted me; this attorney came across like "whatever" when I was with him. I only hope that Chris was having a better conversation with the attorney than I did. Of course, I would have to wait until later to hear from him.

Chris called me, and we compared our thoughts about the meeting. He said his meeting was a little longer than mine but not by much. He was surprised that the attorney met with me first. Chris said that the attorney believed we were on the right track but thought that another controlled call, or better yet a face-to-face visit, would help to seal the case. Chris agreed and mentioned to me that if Paul wanted to meet this time face-to-face since he mentioned over and over again on the first call that we should set it up to happen. He said that he would call me tomorrow to set up a time, and we would try another controlled call and see where that would take us. Chris did agree with me that this attorney was not the friendliest and seemed overly cautious but said we should give him a chance. If he did not feel comfortable with his skills and if I didn't feel better as we progressed, we would request a new attorney. I said we had a deal and I would not let my first impressions get the better of me. That is something that would be hard for me. I am very much a person who judges one by the first impression, but I was willing to try because I believed in Chris and knew that he would know best.

Chapter Fourteen – The Incriminating Call

The next day, June 11, 2002, started out like any other workday. I got my son off to school and then got myself ready to start my day. Work was going good, but I knew that at any time Chris could call, and I would have to confront my molester. I didn't know if I could handle that. At approximately 11:00, the phone rang. Chris wanted me to come to the station and attempt a call and possibly schedule a meeting with Paul.

Shortly thereafter, I was in the phone room with Chris. We attempted to call Paul at home. There was no answer, so we attempted his cell phone with no answer. Finally Chris had me attempt his workplace. The woman that answered said that Paul was on vacation for two weeks. I hung up the phone and stared at Chris.

"What now? What do we do? I guess we have no choice but to wait until he comes back from vacation," I said to Chris with a little disappointment.

"No, I am going to have a car go by the house and see if they really left for a trip. Can you hang out here for a little while?" he asked.

"Sure, I guess."

We decided to wait for a while because I had left Paul a voice mail with a telephone message to call me back, so we wanted to see if he would call. In the meantime, a car drove by the house. No one was home, but for some reason they felt he was still in town. Chris wanted to try again either later in the day or the next morning.

I went home and attempted my usual workday. Every time the phone rang, my heart would skip a beat. I kept expecting each call to be Chris, but to my surprise I ended the whole day and evening without a single call from him. That night my nerves were on edge. I knew that the next day would be it. If Paul were still in town, I would either have to call him or worse yet meet him face to face.

As expected I did get that call from Chris that Paul was home, and he wanted me to come to the station immediately. Once I was there and in the phone room, Chris brought in a female officer. She was going to put a microphone on me to record the conversation and officers in a car were going to watch and videotape me with Paul. All this was being set up just in case Paul mentioned to me that he wanted to meet face to face. We decided that if Paul asked to meet, I would suggest a public park that was close to the police station and even closer to his house. Chris also put together a fake subpoena for me to refer to while talking to Paul. Now all there was to do was call him and see where the conversation was going to take us.

Keep in mind; the following is from the actual police transcript of the controlled call. At times, the conversation may go off track. I guess that is what fear does to someone. I also want to share with you that I was extremely emotional and for some reason really scared when I was making this call.

Paul: Hello
Elaine: Paul?
Paul: Yes.
Elaine: Um, the reason why I'm calling is …Chris Long did get in touch with me the other day at work.
Paul: Yeah.
Elaine: And, out in the parking lot, and I told him I really had nothing to discuss with him and that he should just move on and you know, do an investigation someplace else.
Paul: Yeah.
Elaine: Well the day before yesterday, I was served with a subpoena and I have to go this morning at 11:15 to the State Attorney's Office.
Paul: Do ya, yeah.
Elaine: And I am not happy about this at all.
Paul: Well I'm not either, you know, I didn't do this. Um.
Elaine: You didn't do what?

Paul: What.

Elaine: You didn't do what?

Paul: Well what caused this? What's brought all this up all of a sudden? That's what I'm trying to figure out.

Elaine: Well, whatever you did in March provoked them to come to see me to find about, to find out why, how I can help with this case and we both know how I can help with this case with sexual abuse. Now you're calling me a liar with this and I, I'm scared to go here, you know, I mean, I told you this that I did not want to get involved in this...

Paul: Right.

Elaine: ...at all.

Paul: Right.

Elaine: And now I'm involved in this and it's, I'm rehashing all the things that you had done to me as a child and now, if I don't show up here today it's telling me that I am going to be in contempt of court, which means I go to jail. If I go there and I lie to them, it means I go to jail. Now what do I do?

Paul: Elaine, you know what? You're the sole person that can stand there and say, no, that this did not happen. Leave me alone. They're not gonna push it anymore than that. They're not going to put you under the lights and under the, you know, they're not going to do that. I'm surprised they pushed it this far, you know. But, you're the sole person, Elaine. You gotta be strong, with this if you want to, to help me out. I know you don't, owe me this, and help yourself out. You go in there and you say, no, this did not happen and that's the end of the story. They can't do any more to you than that. You know. If you say, no, even under oath. Elaine, it's not gonna go no further than that, that's it. I'm sorry about the other day when I thought I was being taped. You're the person; you're the key person here.

Elaine: Well, I know.

Paul: And if you go there say this did not happen. We don't know where this came from, or whatever. I don't know where this came from all the sudden. What I'm saying is how will they, how is it now, they've talked to your mom, with papers, all this stuff; they talked to your brother. I don't know where this is coming from. You know, they had to have dug this up somewhere. Right?

Elaine: Somewhere, right.

Paul: Yeah and it's, it's not me. You know I, I wouldn't, I wouldn't do such a stupid thing and, uh, I don't know if you've talked to your brother since this or not. What he says…

Elaine: I haven't talked to him about this at all.

Paul: Yeah.

Elaine: It could be they are fishing for information, um but…

Paul: Yeah.

Elaine: …if you could only hear this Chris Long talk to me, you would swear he knows everything that happened when I was, you know, seven an a half, eight years old up until the day you guys divorced. I mean, he, he is dropping hints to me of things that only you and I would know.

Paul: But see, it's not me that's saying anything. I would not do this, I, I'd is this what you're thinking that I …

Elaine: I don't know and that's why…

Paul: Right.

Elaine: …you know, I'm thinking.

Paul: Right.

Elaine: You know…I don't know if you were under stress, you know, when you were brought in, in March or you know…

Paul: No.

Elaine: Or, if Betty was questioned. Cause, you said that Betty knows things. All I know is that at 11:15 I have to go meet with this person and I don't know what to do.

Paul: Okay, what I would do if you want to, be strong, and just say no. You know. Don't lose it; just be strong, say, no. They're not gonna put you away, Elaine. They're not gonna put you in jail. You're not lying. You know, as far as you…

Elaine: But, you know, you know. You know that even as a kid when I would lie, you and mom knew it because of my body gestures and my eye contact. And I'm thinking, you know, I have been a wreck and I'm…. I don't know how I'm

69

going to go in there and pull myself together and I don't, cuz I don't lie, especially to authority, I mean, that's how I was raised.

Paul: Yeah. Hey, just go over there and be strong for me and please you know, you don't owe me this, but, you can go on with your life after this and I can go on with my life. If this goes through, Elaine, this is going to be bad, not for you but for me.

Elaine: It's gonna be bad for me, too, because I'm gonna be dragged in it with you.

Paul: Yeah.

Elaine: You know I'm gonna have to rehash everything.

Paul: Right. But you...

Elaine: So it's going to be bad, it is going to be bad for a lot of people. I've got a 14-year-old child to think about. What do you think is going to happen to you if this went through?

Paul: Me. If this goes through, Elaine, my life is gone. I, I lose my job. I have to file a chapter, my wife's gonna be on her own and I'm probably facing jail time, you know, four, five, six years of jail time, if this was to go through. My life is done. I'm five years away from retirement with the city and that's gonna be all shot. Its gonna be gone. You know, I'm gonna get out of jail maybe in the mid-sixties or something like that and my life is done, you know, and it's bad enough for me, but like I said to you before, I married a woman who didn't deserve this. Now she's going, we can't even sleep here, you know. We've been up all night thinking why can't Elaine call us, why can't she call us earlier. I don't know what's going on, you know. But...

Elaine: I wasn't going to call you last night from home.

Paul: Right. Yeah, I figured that.

Elaine: You know it's just; I had to come in here today to pick up some paperwork.

Paul: If this, if this goes through, I'm done Elaine. That's it. You know, the city backed me up on that other thing. They stayed behind me and you know I got good news yesterday and bad news, right. They attorney's office calls me yesterday and they're putting a lawsuit together now, a civil lawsuit for these people, I guess. This is great, cause I was accused of something I never did. Right, so I get your message and then we go right down the hole again. Elaine, like I say to you. These fellas, they're not gonna do anything to you. You know.

Elaine: What kind of charges do you think would be against you? I'm…has anybody talked to you about that?

Paul: No, nothing, no, nope. Well, what charge would be against me is whatever you say?

Elaine: Well I mean, I don't know any of this, and on the subpoena it doesn't say anything. It just talks about the investigation, an open investigation, type of thing. It doesn't go into a whole lot of detail.

Paul: Well so you know what; see the police department, Elaine, police. They messed up they probably should never of arrested me and they know this now and they're probably facing a lawsuit too. They should have never arrested me for what happened that night. Never, never, and now cuz we're talking again with… what is going on. Why are they so hot on my case, now? They probably want to get me before I do a lawsuit against them. One way or another, you know, so, that's what's going on. So what time do you have to go again?

Elaine: 11:15.

Paul: Yeah, just pull yourself together, Elaine, they can't do anything to you. They cannot do anything to you. You sit there and you tell, no, it never happened. That's all you tell them. And stick with it. They're not gonna put you under lights, they're not gonna put you on a polygraph machine, they're not gonna call, call you a liar, they're not gonna do this. Just stay calm and say, no. And that way there, it puts an end to this for you and me, you know.

Elaine: Well, when, when you were arrested in March.

Paul: Yeah.

Elaine: Was it, it was a sex charge, then?

Paul: Yeah. Lewd and lascivious. Yep. Yep, and it never happened. I know you don't believe me and I don't expect you to believe me, but it never did happen.

Elaine: Well it's kind of hard to believe you, you know, you have to understand where I'm coming from.

Paul: Right, I know but we got someone here that's little fantasyland and I didn't realize it; these were friends of ours, Elaine. We took them out boating, we did everything with them, you know. So, it never happened.

Elaine: Now I know that you're going on vacation, so I probably can't even call you after I get back from here.

Paul: No, I'll have the cell phone on. We are. Elaine we're so tore up right now, we don't even know if we want to leave, you know. How can you go on vacation at a time like this? We might take a drive; it's not exactly a vacation. It's a combination of other things we have to do. We'll leave the cell phone on. And do me a favor, call me after that, you know. And I don't know why this guy is pursuing something, you know. I don't know what his problem is. We never said anything, I never said anything, and you know what I mean.

Elaine: Right.

Paul: You know, I never have. I never said a word. Why would I be so stupid to go say something like that? But someone has, you know, or someone thinks they know something and they have told, you know, or said something, so.

Elaine: Okay, now just say that, you know, it gets down to, um. I mean I don't know how, if these people are gentle when they are talking to me or if this going to be a hammered kind of conversation. And say that they, um, I say something that leads them to believe this, to know that is sexual thing went on between us. I, then you're gonna end up call…are you gonna call me a liar? If this came to, I know you said that you would face it before and now…

Paul: Elaine, if it comes to that. I'm gonna go down. But, I'm not gonna go down, not fighting back.

Elaine: Right.

72

Paul: You have to understand that part.

Elaine: I just want to know that you're not gonna call me a liar. If something were to happen... (Crying)

Paul: I'm not gonna call you a liar.

Elaine: (Crying)

Paul: But I'm not gonna go down without a fight, Elaine, and you have to understand that part.

Elaine: I know.

Paul: Cause I'm losing my life, okay. That's...

Elaine: I know, like I am too right now. (Crying)

Paul: I, I'm losing my life, you know, I'm losing everything. You know, and if it means I go to jail, then I go to jail but you know. I feel bad for a wife I have here. You know so. What I would do as far as you just stay strong, you know and tell them, no, and no, and no and if they keep it up. You're going to hire a lawyer and sue them for harassment, you know.

Elaine: I just don't want any part of this.

Paul: No, I don't either and I don't blame you. You know.

Elaine: But you know, all I've been thinking about since I had this subpoena is all the things that had taken place from when I was seven and a half, eight years old right up until the day that I moved out, you know, and its just like. I've had nightmares. I can't stop thinking about this, you know. I think even, do you know, the one event that like has the most impact, I think is. When we first moved here and I had to perform oral sex on you and that is all I've been thinking about, since this stupid frickin piece of paper showed up at my door.

Paul: That did not happen.

Elaine: Whatever. Okay, Paul...

Paul: I'm not...,

Elaine: ...I, you think I'm going to forget this thing. I remember you would not believe the stuff I can remember. The smells...

Paul: Okay.

Elaine: ...the touches, the things, everything.

Paul: Okay, it did happen, Elaine what you're saying, but it wasn't there.

Elaine: Yes, it was there.

Paul: Okay, anyway, you know, but like I say you know. I'm gonna give it a fight too, you know. You know, cause I'm losing my life. You know, at 57, I'm losing, everything is going down.

Elaine: Well, I feel like that's how things are going for me right now. They've been going wonderful for me and now I've had this thing thrown at me.

Paul: I didn't say anything to anyone.

Elaine: But you did in a sense, indirectly then you did because of whatever other charges have been brought against you this is obviously made them want...

Paul: What, what I'm saying is what gives them the idea to go to you after that?

Elaine: I don't know.

Paul: That is what I'm asking. You know, I'm wondering. I keep wondering what is it, who said something, it wasn't me.

Elaine: Well, I gotta get going. I got, um, I just came here to work to pick up some papers and I gotta get ready for this appointment.

Paul: Alright. Well can you just hold strong, Elaine, and just say, no? And then, you know, you come out of there say no, Elaine, just remember it's the end for both of us, you know. You don't owe me that, but, I'm begging you, you know. Just go in there and say no. Like I said they're not going...

Elaine: Then you're telling me to lie...then I feel like I'm being told that I'm, that I'm a liar or I'm going to be a liar and...I don't, I'm gonna have to think about this. I don't know. But I can't make any promises. I mean, I'm gonna go in there just like you said my first intention is to protect my child and me.

Paul: Right.

Elaine: And that's what I'm gonna do. And, um, but I just wanted to let you know what is going on, and, um, I need to get going, cause like I said I don't even, I'm here before anybody is even in the office. I just want to get my stuff and get out.

Paul: Elaine, listen to me, if you just say no that's the end of the story. They're not gonna lock you up, they're not gonna call you a liar, they're not… You're the key pin, if you say, no, that's it, just stay strong, say no, its all over. Just say, no. They're not going to lock you up, Elaine. Not you. You know, they're not gonna put you on a polygraph test, they're not gonna put you under hot lights. Just stay calm, and say, no. Just keep me in mind, it never happened.

Elaine: But you don't know that for sure, you don't know, I mean.

Paul: They can't push you anymore than that. You're the key pin, you're the one. If you don't press charges, if you say, no. It's, it's done for, and it's over.

Elaine: But I'm not pressing charges. It's not a thing for me to go and press charges…

Paul: Alright.

Elaine: …it's to answer questions.

Paul: To answer questions. You just say, no. Its simple enough Elaine, just say, no. You know, did he ever do this, no, did he ever do this, no. You know, that's the end of story. That's it, they can threaten you. They can do whatever…

Elaine: So lie, I'm just gonna have to go in there and lie.

Paul: Well, if, if you want to go that route it'd be a lot better for all of us. You know. It'd be better than the other way we're gonna go. And then it's over. You know, you don't ever have to talk to me. I'll never forget you, I told you that the other day. I'll never forget you. You know. I still love you to this day like I did back then.

Elaine: Well, I gotta go, um, there's somebody out there, so I, like I said, I just wanted to get my stuff.

Paul: Alright. Please, I'm begging you. You don't owe me this, but just go in there and say, no to everything. Please. And it's over with. They can't do anything to you, Elaine. They won't do anything to you, you know. Please. Just compose yourself, its no, simple. You're not up for a murder trial; you're not going to jail. I am. You know. It's simple. No, no, and no, you know. No, leave me alone, if you don't leave me alone I'm gonna hire an attorney and I'm gonna sue you for harassment. And that's the end of story.

Elaine: Alright, well, I gotta go.

Paul: Alright, can you promise me, something though?

Elaine: What?

Paul: Will you call after that and let me know?

Elaine: Yes.

Paul: We're gonna hang around, I cant leave here now. I'm all tore up too, you know.

Elaine: Alright, I'll call you. (crying) Bye.

Paul: Hey Elaine.

Elaine: What?

Paul: Good luck, okay.

Elaine: Yeah, bye.

Paul: Bye.

End of the second control phone call.

Chris and I looked at each other; we both had tears in our eyes. He held my hand tight, and he just thanked me over and over and commented how well the call went. The female detective that was going to wire me up if I ended up meeting Paul in person was also choked up; she just put her hand on my shoulder. Both Chris and the detective told me that this tape was enough and they were going to arrest him that day.

Chris walked me to my car and gave me a warm and caring hug; he spoke softly and asked if I was going to be okay to drive home. I just nodded yes. I left the parking lot and called my mother. I fell apart on the phone talking to her. I filled her in as much as possible but felt so emotionally exhausted that I just needed to go home.

Once I was at home, I went into the bathroom and got sick. I sat on the couch for a very long time in total silence. I just kept hearing Paul's voice telling me over and over to get it together and just say no, that nothing happened. All he cared about was himself and his precious wife. I couldn't believe it. Now all I had to do was wait to find out when Paul would be taken into custody.

Chapter Fifteen – The Arrest

I was finally able to control myself and get a grip on what had just taken place. I knew that what I did was the right thing. Paul needed to be punished for what he had done to me and to those other innocent children. The phone rang about one hour after I got home and it was Chris.

"Hey, Elaine, I'm in my car in front of Paul's house. I'm watching our officers' knock on the door. He's opening the door. He's stepping outside. He's turning around. The handcuffs are being put on him. He's walking to the police car. He's getting in. His wife is just standing there. He's in the car. They are driving away. You did it, Elaine, we got him. Now I'm going back to the station to question him. I will call you later."

That was it Chris hung up. He'd given me a play-by-play of the whole thing, and I never said a word.

I called my mother and told her what had just happened. She was shocked but glad something positive had happened. I was shaking and I felt cold and extremely nervous. I had so many emotions running through me at once--fear, sadness, and happiness--I was just so overwhelmed. It seemed like hours before my phone rang, but when it did, my heart skipped a beat. It was Chris. He had just finished interrogating Paul. Chris said that it went pretty much the way he expected. Chris said that Paul lied a lot through the interrogation. Of course it is all on tape, and the jury will love to see how he lies. When Paul was asked if he had recently spoken to me, he said he hadn't. Over and over again, Chris gave him the chance to change his mind. Paul just kept denying that we had spoken to one another.

Chris let me know that Paul left the police station and was on his way to county lock-up. He said I did great and once Paul was processed, he would let me know in case I wanted to go to the bond hearing, which would more than likely be the next day.

I called my mother and told her about the interrogation. She said that she had found work coverage and would be heading home right away. When my mother got home, we both sat and cried. My mother was so wonderful. She was so supportive and caring. She said that now we would wait for Chris to call to get the information about attending the bond hearing. I decided that I wanted to speak at the hearing, so I wrote down what I wanted to say. I knew that I would be extremely nervous so, I had to have something prepared.

Paul was arrested on June 12, 2002. The bond hearing was the morning of June 13, 2002. The morning of June 13 was a long one. My mother, brother, and his wife went with me to the bond hearing. I was told to let the bailiff know that I was there and that I wanted to speak. My nerves were so on edge; I could feel myself coming apart. Then I saw Paul's wife and a friend. They were giving me such horrible looks, I felt very intimidated by them. I was also extremely concerned because no one from state side asked to speak with me before Paul's hearing.

Paul's attorney got up in front of the judge and spoke about the charges being false and how Paul was such a wonderful person and an asset to the community.

The judge asked if anyone wanted to get up and speak at that time. I stood up and so did Paul's wife and friend. All three of us were up in front of the judge. I went first and said the following:

"Your honor, my name is Elaine Carole, and I am here today to plea to you to keep this man, Paul Carole, here and without bond. I am afraid of this man and fear what he might do to me for coming forward with this horrible secret I have kept from my family. This man has not only violated me sexually, he violated the trust and love that a father and daughter should share. I should have been able to trust this man to protect me from such harm, but instead he was the one inflicting harm on me and I was too afraid and ashamed to ask others for protection from him.

Since Sgt. Chris Long came to my home on May 23rd, I have been forced to relive the sexual abuse all over again. I was only seven years old when this man came to my room to show me how 'special' I was. This 'affection', as Paul calls it, continued until I was almost 18 years old. At the request of the police department, I did two controlled phone calls to Paul from the police station where Paul admitted to sexually abusing me and asked me to lie for him. He even shared with me that his current wife was aware of what he had done to me as a child. Since this investigation, I have been afraid to be alone. These horrible events that took place when I was a child have consumed me. I walk around my own house afraid and always carrying a phone in case Paul shows up. I cannot sleep at night and when I do finally fall asleep, I have horrible nightmares. My work performance is also suffering.

"I am a single parent of a 14-year-old son, and I fear for his safety. I have seen first-hand what this man is capable of when he is full of rage and anger. I feel I have every right to fear him now, especially after breaking my silence of what this man did to me as a child. Please take my feelings and fear for both my child and myself into consideration before posting any type of bond or release of this man. Thank you for your time."

I was shaking so hard, I could feel my knees wanting to give out. I stepped back, and then Paul's wife and friend spoke on his behalf. They spoke about how wonderful Paul was and what a great husband and friend he was. The whole thing was rather sickening.

When it was all said and done, the state said it was asking for $10,000 bond, since they really didn't review the case. I wanted to scream. I couldn't believe this woman, this attorney supposedly representing me, was only asking for $10,000 bond, when he got a $50,000 bond the last time he was arrested. I felt robbed. I felt that this case was quickly going down the drain, and the fight that Paul said he was going to give, well; at that point, I thought for sure he was going to win.

The judge did order Paul and his friends not to have any direct or indirect contact with anyone in my family, but that didn't make me feel any safer. I really felt that if he wanted to hurt me or scare me, he would do it no matter what. To me the judge's verbal warning meant nothing.

The ride home was extremely long and quiet. My mother and I were at a loss for words. I felt so defeated; I had no energy or desire to say anything. I just felt such fear inside and knew now that Paul would get me and it wasn't going to be good.

Chapter Sixteen – New Friends Come to Support Me

A couple of days had passed, and I was still feeling down. I spoke with Chris and told him what had happened. He was as disappointed with the outcome as I, but he still was able to remain positive and hopeful. I will always be thankful for that in him.

I also contacted my attorney and I told him about his partner who was representing the state at the time and how let down I felt. He was in total shock. He had no idea that Paul was even out of jail, let alone on a $10,000 bond. I could hear and feel his rage and disappointment in his co-worker. He told me not to worry and quickly hung up.

I could feel the depression setting in. I was crying all the time and feeling scared, and I couldn't get out of it. This was more than I could handle. I was already feeling I couldn't go through with this. Chris was going to have to do it without me. I was ready to let Paul win--again.

It was then I got a surprise call from Chris. He told me that some neighbors of Paul's really wanted to talk to me. They wanted to thank me and let me know that they were behind me one hundred percent. He gave me a telephone number of one of the neighbors. He said that when I was ready to call her, I could relax because she was a very nice person; all of the women who wanted to speak with me were wonderful. I held on to the number for a couple of days and then decided to call Gerri. As Chris said, she was so nice. She told me about her kids and how they were not directly affected by Paul but her best friend's daughter was. She kept saying how brave I was and how proud they all were of me. It was amazing and strange to hear these words coming from a stranger. We spoke several times, and then I called Gerri's friend, K.C. We had a nice conversation. I was comfortable talking with them, and I think they felt the same way. In the meantime, two friends joined in, so now I had four new wonderful friends on my side that lived in Paul's neighborhood. Two of them lived either right next door or across the street. They made me feel like I had known them forever.

The women wanted to meet my mother and me; we had all spoken so much on the phone, we thought it might be nice to meet one another. They had all decided that they would attend every pre-trial or anything that happened, so it only made sense to meet me. We all met for lunch, at an Italian restaurant, and we sat in a private corner where we could be alone. We hugged one another as we met. Once we were all together, they all introduced themselves and shared how their children were victims of Paul. The stories were sad, and tears fell from all of us. I was able to share some things with them and my mother also told them things that I just couldn't. The meeting was good and a lot of tears were shed, but it was great to put a face to these stories I had heard either over the phone or by Chris. They all vowed to attend the pre-trial hearing and promised to attend everything no matter what; they were going to be there to support me. That was a wonderful feeling; it was the shot in the arm I needed.

A day or two later, Chris called me and said that a reporter from our major newspaper wanted to print an article about the recent arrest. He promised to leave my name out of it. Chris thought this article should be published because it might help to bring out more victims that may have lived in the neighborhood at one time or another. I agreed and asked Chris to make sure my name was left out; after all I was trying to protect my son from this.

Chris called me a couple of days later. "Did you see the article in the paper today?"

"No, is it good?" I replied.

"Yes, he did a great job, and I think it may touch people out there," he said.

"Well, I'm going to go get the paper right now, and I'll call you later," I said. We said our good-byes and hung up. I agreed with Chris. The article was done in great taste. The reporter kept his promise and left my name out of it.

Man accused of sexually abusing relative

- *Police are searching for other potential victims.*

Police have arrested a man on suspicion he sexually abused a relative in the 1970s. Investigators now are looking to see if he may have abused other children.

Paul Carole, 57 was arrested on a capital sexual battery charge Wednesday. He was being held at the county jail Thursday in lieu of $10,000 bail.

Carole, a supervisor in the city's solid waste department, also arrested in March on a charge that he molested a young neighborhood girl. Prosecutors later dropped the charge because of inconsistent testimony from the young victim and a young witness, said the state attorney.

Children also accused Carole of improperly touching and kissing them in 1994, but there wasn't enough evidence to charge him with a crime, said Sgt. Chris Long.

He denied abusing any children during both investigations.

But now police are searching for other potential victims, Long said.

"Once, then twice, that's going to send up flags to any law enforcement agency that there may be an issue there," Long said. "There is concern there may be other victims that we don't know about."

"When prosecutors dropped the first charge against Carole, police continued to investigate him, partially spurred by phone calls from neighbors who suspected him of child sex abuse," Long said.

Long contacted the relative's family. The relative later told Long that Carole had sexual intercourse with her many times and that the sexual abuse continued for about 10 years, Long said.

"He did make a statement indicating he had sexual contact with the victim," Long said.

Long said anyone with information can call police at 555-1212.

This article did spark a lot of interest, but no one else came forward. I don't know if that made me happy or sad. I know there could be other victims out there that were just terrified to come forward. I know because I was one of those victims and in some sense still was. The neighbors in Paul's neighborhood were thankful for the article and were also hoping that maybe others would come forward.

Some of the women in the neighborhood suspected that a boy that lived near Paul could have been another potential victim, but family refused to talk to anyone about it. The boy asked a lot of questions to the neighbors in regards to the arrest and almost seemed relieved of the arrest.

Chapter Seventeen – It's Time to Tell the Family

With all of the events that had been going on, my mother and I decided that it would probably be a good idea to bring my aunts, uncles, and cousins up to speed. The only problem was I didn't want any part of it. I had no problem with everyone in my family knowing, but I just couldn't be the one to do the telling. My mother agreed to do it for me. She called an aunt and uncle that live locally and asked if she could get together with them. She asked if possible whether my two cousins could also be present. They agreed and asked what was wrong; she only told them that Paul had done something really bad.

The next night my mother nervously went over to see my relatives. She was gone for a very long time. Apparently, when my aunt shared with my cousins that my mother was coming over to discuss something Paul had done, they decided to look up the local newspaper web site to see if they could find anything on him. Of course they found the article, but things just didn't seem to register that it was me. Once my mother told them, they were all extremely distraught and overwhelmed. My one cousin seemed to take it the hardest. Although we are about six years apart, we have always been close. He is a very loving and caring person. My mother told me that he was beside himself and could barely control his saddened emotions.

My other cousin who is closer in age with me decided to leave the meeting with my mother and come directly to my house. She and I grew up together and shared a lot of secrets, but this is one she knew nothing about. I could see the sadness in her eyes before she even said a word. We talked together for about an hour and held hands and hugged a lot. It was a great comfort to know that the family was going to stand with me through this whole ordeal. Not that I doubted it, but it is nice to have that reassurance. All of them agreed not to mention this to any of the other members in the family. The rest of them were out of state, so contacting them with this news was going to have to be properly timed.

When my mother came home from my relatives', she looked extremely drained both mentally and physically. She said that all of them were deeply sorry and would do whatever needed to help us get through this. The next night my mother called two of my uncles and my other aunt, all of whom are in different states. I could hear her crying as she was telling them what was going on. All of them, again like the others, promised to pray and do whatever they could to help me through this horrible time.

I think deep down they were a little scared, too, and I think they were nervous to talk to me. I don't know if they thought I was going to be different or what, but it was weird. It was almost like talking to someone after a loved one has died; no one really knows what to say.

A few days had passed, and my cousin called me. He wanted me to meet him for dinner at a local restaurant. I agreed and was glad to see him. We had a great conversation before and all through dinner. We spoke of our kids, work, and school. We had a lot of great laughs.

When it came to dessert the mood quickly changed. We were sitting across from each other and he was holding my hands. The tears were falling so fast and hard from his eyes that his sadness caused me to do the same thing. All this was happening before we even said a word. He then shared that he had been sick with grief ever since my mother told him of the news; he actually started to blame himself. He kept saying that he should have seen something. I tried to assure him that this man was good at what he did, that no one would have ever known or found out. Even my own mother didn't know. The last thing he or anyone should be doing is to blame themselves. He knew I was right, but he was just so hurt. When he was younger, he was around and did things with Paul and my brother. This was the last thing he ever expected to hear.

We wiped our tears and tried to laugh as we shared a great dessert together. He walked me to my car and we hugged and said our good-byes. I sat in my car for a while before I even started it. I was so overwhelmed by his reaction, and I didn't know what to do. I did know this. I was truly loved by my family, and I was lucky.

A couple of days later, my aunt and uncle that my mother went to talk with came by for a visit. My aunt looked so sad, and she also looked like she had not slept. Again, we all carried on positive conversations, but we did a lot of hand- holding and hugging.

It was a little odd and uncomfortable talking over the phone to my aunt and uncles that live in other states. It was as if they were afraid to say the wrong thing, or maybe they were afraid I would go off the deep end and go crazy. Once we began our conversations, they knew that it was still me, and they could still tease me and give me the usual hard times. I did get a beautiful card from one of my aunts, and I have to say that it came at a time when I really needed the extra pick-me-up. I always knew I had a wonderful loving family, but seeing them all coming to my aid was just the added proof I needed during this trying time.

Chapter Eighteen – May the Delays Begin

Two months has passed since the bond hearing. Life for me was not totally back to normal, but I sure tried to make it that way. I was scared all the time, I couldn't sleep at night, and I feared being alone during the day. Each night, I would lie in bed and my mind began to play tricks on me. I would hear things outside and believe someone was breaking in. It became so out of control that we needed to install a house alarm. The alarm helped some but didn't totally take my fears away. I would watch the clock each night and just wait for the day to start. When I did sleep at night, I would dream that the doorbell would ring. I would answer it, and Paul would be at the door with a gun and shoot me over and over again in the stomach. I would wake up in cold sweats and end up with pounding headaches everyday. During the day, I would not go anywhere without either my cell phone or portable phone. When I shower, I would take both of them with me into the bathroom.

On August 23, 2002 I had to appear at the courthouse for a deposition with my attorney and Paul's attorney. I went with my victim advocate that was assigned to me by the police department. We were there on time and waited for Paul's attorney. My attorney was down the hall doing some paperwork while we waited for the other attorney. Finally, about thirty minutes later, Paul's attorney showed up. It turns out he "forgot" to order the court reporter. He tried to blame it on his office staff, but my advocate and I truly believed that it was a mind game he was playing with us. After sitting for about two hours waiting for nothing, we rescheduled the appointment and went on our way.

Paul's attorney appeared to be fresh out of law school. He came across as either tough or a "Mr. Know-it-all," when all he really did was show his inexperience and lack of maturity. Other attorneys made jokes about him and no one seemed to take him seriously.

I went home after that waste of time and felt very angry. I was so calm and ready for this to take on whatever questions that were going to be thrown at me.

On the 26th of August, the first pre-trial took place. As promised, all of my new friends from Paul's neighborhood, my aunt, uncle, cousins, mother, brother, and his wife were present to support me. It was great to have so many people sitting on the prosecution side for me. Of course Paul's attorney got up and asked for a continuation since all depositions were not completed. My attorney got up and really didn't fight it. The judge asked the victim to stand up, and, when I stood up, all of my supporters also stood up. It was impressive to have so many people backing me up, when Paul only had a couple. The judge granted the postponement. I felt so defeated; it felt like Paul was winning again. First, he got a super low bail, and then he got a delay. I had such a hard time with this, but according to my advocate, this was normal. She said it wouldn't be unusual to have two or three pre-trial motions. This seemed unfair to me, and I couldn't believe that as a victim my feelings and fears were not being considered.

On September 6, 2002 I again went back to the court-house for another deposition. Again my victim advocate went with me. This time it started right on time. The funny thing was I was not at all scared or frightened. I guess when you are telling the truth, there is nothing to be afraid of, so the calmness that had come over me wasn't really a surprise. In a very small room at an extremely small desk were my attorney, Paul's attorney, the court reporter and I. My advocate sat off to the side. All introductions were made and then we got down to business. I was told not to answer the questions right away that I needed to allow my attorney to object if needed. I folded my hands in front of me and sat up straight, as I looked Paul's attorney right in the eye. I was seeing what others had said about Paul's attorney. Basically he was being a real jerk. Right in the middle of a deep conversation, all of the sudden he asked to go off the record because he wanted to tell us a joke. When he noticed that no one really cared to hear it, he said we were no fun and went back on record. Things like this happened throughout the whole deposition. When it was over, I felt great. I knew I had done a great job. I had told the truth and that was all that mattered.

When I got home, I called my mother. I then called Chris and told him about how unprofessional the attorney was acting. He was glad to have the heads up because he was up next for the deposition. I also called the women from the neighborhood and filled them in. Everyone was proud of me and said wonderful things.

After hanging up, I started to feel all the same old emotions, sadness, fear and severe anxiety. These emotions were consuming me and getting extremely out of control. It ended up that I had to go see my doctor. I am normally a very healthy person. I don't take any medications, and I don't even take aspirin when I have a headache. Seeing this doctor made me feel like, once again Paul was winning. I was forced to see a doctor because I couldn't keep my emotions in tact. The doctor did a full check-up including my blood pressure. I filled him in on everything that was going on. After spending more than an hour with him, he decided that I really needed to be on blood pressure medication and something for depression. This upset me severely and, in the beginning, I was not very open to taking them. I started taking them only every once in a while, but soon my depression was more than I could handle. Functioning daily became harder, so I knew that I had to take the medication. I began to tell myself that it was only temporary. I knew that I would not need this medication forever.

The medication took some time to work, but when it did I felt a little better. The days didn't seem so long or so sad, but the nights were still a challenge. I just couldn't get a grip at night. Although I believe in God, I don't usually pray or attend church regularly, but I found myself praying every night. I asked for strength and begged for justice to prevail in my favor.

On October 7, 2002, we went again for another pre-trial and again the court granted Paul another delay. I just couldn't believe it. Once again, Paul was getting everything, and I was getting nothing. The system just didn't seem fair. Even though all the same supporters showed up for me, I felt so alone. I didn't have my advocate with me because she had retired. Another one had not yet been assigned on to my case. The courthouse had an advocate on hand and she attended the pre-trial, but since I didn't know her, I didn't ask her anything. I just left the courthouse with the feeling of defeat as Paul walked out with his wife by his side and his head held high.

I had to continue my visits to my doctor because my blood pressure was still out of control. With the holidays upon us, all the pre-trials would be scheduled after the New Year. For now, it was delay after delay. The score was Paul 3 and me nothing.

Chapter Nineteen – Tis' the Season

Thanksgiving was upon us, and my mother, son, and I decided to head to Las Vegas for seven days. It was a great distraction and we did a lot of planning to make it a wonderful trip. My son and I planned to visit a lot of wonderful places while in Vegas. Gambling is not my thing, but I was in Vegas for a sales meeting the year before and loved it. Going back with my family was going to be wonderful. While in Vegas, we rented a car and drove all over we even went into Utah.

We visited all the wonderful hotels, attended a great show, and ate at the most fabulous places. The ultimate was a helicopter tour that my son and I went on. My uncle who is out of state sent me a note with a check attached telling me to have a wonderful trip. We took the helicopter over the Hoover Dam, over an extinct volcano, and landed in the Grand Canyon, where a chuck wagon picked us up and took us to a working Dude Ranch. We had lunch with cowboys, rode on horses, and then, to top it off, it started to snow. It was beautiful. The whole week was wonderful, and for the first time in several months, I felt safe. I didn't even think about what I was facing at home.

When I got home, it was time to get ready for Christmas. I still had shopping to do and decorations to hang outside. My son and I love to decorate the house. We put up lots of lights and mechanical reindeer. The lights looked beautiful, and I was feeling pretty good. Don't get me wrong. I still had my moments, but it was nice to have so much to keep me busy.

A couple of weeks before Christmas we had our usual open house, which always it turns out to be wonderful. This year was especially nice. We invited the women from Paul's neighborhood and their husbands, my relatives, and other close friends. We agreed we were not going to discuss the case or Paul. This was a party, and we were going to have fun. It was wonderful! We had a great evening and, again, my mind was on the party and nothing else.

I had a great Christmas day with my family. It was very relaxing, and we just stayed home and enjoyed each other. It really was what holidays are all about-- being with loved ones. My mother gave me a very special gift for Christmas-- a diamond ring with three diamonds, one representing the past, one representing the present, and one representing the future. It is beautiful. I look at it all the time and feel warm all over when I do, knowing it came from her with such love. She said that she felt I deserved something special since I have been having such a hard time. I felt the tears building in my eyes, and all I could think to do was to hug her. A new year was here, and I was full of hope that this year would be on my side and that justice would be with me one hundred percent.

In January, I went camping for my birthday, just like I do each year. When I was first making the plans, I wasn't sure if I wanted to go. My thoughts were starting to come back to the case and Paul on a regular basis. Then the thought of leaving my mother home alone scared me. I was still convinced that Paul was going to hurt us. My mother convinced me to go, and I was glad that she did. I had the best time with my son. We did a lot of fishing, walking, and cooking great foods. For those couple of days, it was nice to be alone with my son and to not think of anything but having a great time with him.

Once the holidays were over and my birthday was behind me, it was back to getting ready for a trial. Of course, the fear returned without any delay.

A lot of time was passing, and the case seemed to be dragging on, in my eyes anyway. I was assigned a new advocate. Her name was Karen. She was wonderful; she was my age and seemed to really know the system and how it worked. I was able to ask her all types of questions as to what to expect. She also helped me to better understand my attorney. I needed an attorney who was both understanding and comforting, but my attorney was neither of those. She told me that she had worked with him in the past and that he was not known for those characteristics. She did say, however, that he was great in court and had a terrific winning record. That made me feel a little better.

Now it was just a waiting game. Would Paul want to plea out or was he going to take it to trial? Family and friends were all predicting that Paul would plea out. One person even thought he might take off. I, on the other hand, knew that Paul would want to take this all the way to trial. Maybe he hoped I would drop out just as I hoped he would.

Chapter Twenty – Emotions are high with Terror

We were well into May with another pre-trial under-way. My emotions were becoming more out of control. It had been almost one year since my visit with Chris that turned my world upside down.

My attorney had called me to ask me some questions about when I was a kid. The way he would ask the questions always made me feel like I had to defend myself. I hated that feeling, but I kept thinking about Karen and what she said. After the call with him, I was again all worked up. I was feeling angry and scared. Why is he treating me like this? Doesn't he believe me? If he doesn't believe me, will the court and the jury? I asked myself these questions over and over. I hated having these questions and feelings, but I didn't know how to shake them.

On May 13, 2003, we went for another pre-trial and once again, the judge allowed Paul's attorney to have another delay. I was furious, but I wasn't the only one. All of Paul's neighbors and my relatives were full of rage, too. Once again this molester was getting all the rights and I, the victim, apparently had none. This wasn't fair. Why doesn't the system care about me? Why does Paul have all the rights? These were questions that no one could answer to my satisfaction.

My fear was still high at home. I didn't feel safe; I was still having nightmares and not sleeping at all. I figured that maybe I needed to try to get back to a more normal routine. I have always loved working in the yard; I take great pride in my home, so I decided that I would get out there and do some weeding and cut the grass. Paul works for the department of the City that oversees sanitation, the same service that picks up my trash. While outside working on the yard one morning, a trash truck pulled up almost in front of my home. The men inside just sat in the truck and stared at me. It wasn't the usual crew that picks up our trash, and for that matter, our trash had already been picked up. They just sat in front watching me. At first it really scared me, and I went inside and watched them, but they wouldn't leave. I told my mother what I thought was going on. She wanted to call the police but I disagreed. I decided to go back out and just ignore them. I could feel them watching me, but I held strong and stayed out there and worked on my yard. Eventually they left and when they did, I got the truck number. I then called Chris and told him what happened. He promised he would take care of it. I don't know what he did, but I never again had a truck park in front of my home.

Since I wasn't sleeping at night, I would try to get a little rest after my son left for school. About 8:30 one morning, while I was lying down, the phone rang. It was my uncle who lives here locally. He wanted to know how I was doing; I guess he could hear it in my voice that things really weren't going well. I was full of fear and depression. We talked for a while and then I told him I really needed to get started with work. After hanging up, I decided to color my hair. I had about ten minutes left before removing the color when the phone rang again. It was my uncle calling back, this time to say that he was picking me up in about one hour, to go to lunch and he wasn't going to take no for an answer. I quickly washed the color out of my hair out and got ready for my uncle. He was right on schedule and we were off. We stopped by my cousin's business to say hello and ask him if he wanted to join us. He decided to join us, and we were going to this great hot dog joint. It was a small hole in the wall but had the best hot dogs ever. The three of us jumped in my uncle's Rodeo and we were off for a hot dog frenzy. That was the best day ever. The two of them had me laughing the whole time, and not once was Paul brought up in the conversation. For those couple of hours, my troubles were in the back of my mind and being with those two guys, having great laughs, and stuffing ourselves with a lot of hot dogs was the best distraction ever. I hated to see that day end, but I knew I had to get back to work and try to come to terms with my fears. For the rest of the day though, I was able to think about those two wonderful guys who really care about me. They were able to free me from my fears, even if it was only temporarily.

Time was continuing to pass but not the stress level. I knew that eventually we would have to go to a trial. I knew that Paul would never plea out. On June 11, 2003, I met with my attorney. This time Karen was with me, so my fear was a little less. We met in a small conference room. My nerves started to take over a little, and I found myself building up tears. I shared with my attorney how he made me feel. He actually looked surprised but then smiled a little and said, "Good." The tension was broken and we had a successful meeting. He told me that we were going to have another pre-trial but that this would be the last one. Since Paul's attorney left the firm he was associated with, the judge would allow time for preparation. Carl, my attorney, said he wasn't going to fight it. He didn't want to do anything to cause a mistrial or appeal.

As planned, we went to the pre-trial on June 24, 2003, and the judge set a date for trial. A little bit of argument ensued about the date for trial but finally all agreed on August 7, 2003. I had less than two months to prepare myself mentally for trial. Who knows? Maybe everyone was right. Maybe Paul would plea out. Carl, of course, didn't want a plea offer. He wanted to fight it out, but if I was offered a deal, he had to present it to me.

I had to continue taking my medication because I was still having a lot of severe anxiety, not to mention the fear I was experiencing. I was still having the same nightmare. Paul shoots me over and over again in the stomach when I open the door. I no longer wanted to be home alone nor had the desire to go anywhere.

I had a lot of vacation time accumulated at work, so a vacation was well needed and deserved. Because my son was involved in a local fishing tournament, going out of state was totally out of the question. I decided that what I needed was to spend some time on the beach with a good book and great music in my headset. I rented a place for a week on the beach, which was only about ten minutes from my home. I had a great time; I didn't allow myself to think about the upcoming trial. I wanted to enjoy my time relaxing on the beach and swimming in the pool. My son enjoyed his time fishing in the tournament, and my mother was able to join us after work. It was great and more importantly it was just what I needed. I was able to forget all about the terror that was going on in my life.

All too soon, I was home again and time was closing in to the big day. I was hard at work on Friday, August 1, when all of the sudden I started feeling a panic attack; I had to call my uncle who lives in the Carolinas. He answered the phone and I started to cry. I told him about my fear and thought calling him would be the best medicine. He was good for a great laugh. He then told me not to worry because he was canceling his plans for another trip. Instead he was going to drive down to be with me during the trial. He would be here on Wednesday, the 6th. I was so happy; I thanked him and told him I couldn't wait. I hung up with him and called my mother. I told her what my uncle was going to do, and she was pleasantly surprised. She called my uncle that night and thanked him.

On August 5, 2003, I met with Carl and Karen. Carl wanted to prep me for trial. I wasn't sure what to expect. I have never done anything like this and I had only seen it on television. In some sense, it was a lot like television, but the big difference was it was happening to me, not some television star.

This time Carl was different. He seemed to be very caring and extremely focused on me, and that is what I needed. He went over some questions that he would be asking me. He then shared with me what I could and couldn't say. The important thing was not to mention the kids in Paul's neighborhood. That case could not be discussed at all, which made it a little difficult to word how I would explain how Sgt. Chris Long and I came to meet. Carl said that the jury would figure out that there was more to the story, but we were not at liberty to discuss it. We were counting on the jury being smart and paying attention.

I was with Carl and Karen for about one hour and it was mentally draining. Carl decided that we should meet again the next day before the trial. We said our good-byes and then Karen and I left. We had a great discussion; she was extremely surprised that Carl set up another meeting.

"Do you realize that he never does that? You must be getting to him, Elaine," said Karen.

"I can't believe it either. I have to tell you though, Karen, I have never felt this good. I wish we were going to trial right now," I replied. Then I started wondering if he wanted to see me again because he thought I was doing terrible and I needed all the help I could get. Karen reassured me that was not the case at all. She thought I was doing great, and the nice thing about Karen was that she was honest. If she thought I needed more help, she would say so.

The 6th of August was going to be a busy one. I had my meeting again with Carl and Karen, and then Karen offered to meet with everyone attending the trial to coach them on proper court behavior and how the day was expected to play out. The meeting with Carl and Karen went great. Carl was extremely caring, and my confidence level was once again rising. Carl sat across from me and held my hand. He answered any questions I had and expressed that we were going to be fine the next day for trial. He then had to leave the room for a moment; he was going to get me copies of my deposition, and when he returned he was grinning. He said that he ran into Paul's attorney who wanted to know if we would be interested in a plea of three years' probation. Carl said he just laughed at him. He said he couldn't tell me what his response was to Paul's attorney because I was a lady. Carl told me that when we go to trial, he was going for a sentence of life in prison. I just said, "Yeah, okay" not thinking this was for real. But Carl was serious.

As promised, my uncle arrived from the Carolinas. I was so happy to see him. We hung out at my house for a while and then made plans for lunch. We met up with my other uncle and my cousin. We went to a little deli for a sandwich and a lot of laughs. The support from these three was awesome and just what I needed.

That night at 7:00, Karen met with approximately twenty people, all of whom were attending the trial the next day. We met in a private room in the back of a coffee house for about two hours. Karen was able to go through the whole day using a time line. She suggested that everyone come around 1:00 in the afternoon. There was no point in coming any sooner as the trial most likely would not start until around 2:00 p.m. everyone asked a lot of great questions and most importantly promised to be on their best courtroom behavior.

Around 9:30, my mother and I said our good nights. Everyone hugged me and thanked me again for what I was doing. Once we got home, my mother and I changed into comfortable clothes and decided to watch TV and relax. The night turned out to be rather long. I was in bed for the longest time before falling asleep; of course, when I did finally fall asleep; I had that usual horrible nightmare.

In the morning it was business as usual. I had to get my son breakfast and off to school. I reminded him that I would not be home when he got home from school. He was to come in, fix himself something to eat, or, if he wanted, he could ride his bike over to McDonald's. Then he was to do any homework he might have and watch T.V. For dinner he could order in Chinese food. Under no circumstances was he allowed to have any guests in the house. He was fine with that. I told him I would call him during breaks. All this time, my son had no idea what was going on. I told him I was going to a seminar for work, and his grandmother was going to join me.

After he left for school, I finished getting myself ready, ate a piece of toast, and then we left for the courthouse. This was going to be the longest day of my life and an extremely trying one. I was hoping all the friends and family would be as confident and supportive as always, but I was also hoping God would be watching over me that day.

Chapter Twenty-One – Morning of the Trial

My mother and I met with Karen at the courthouse at 7:45 a.m. I was trying to remain calm, but I knew that the morning would be long without much happening, but my heart was beating at an extremely fast rate.

The three of us went straight to the state attorney's office as summoned by my subpoena. I checked in with the receptionist and then took a seat until my name was called. We sat there until about 8:20 a.m., and finally they called my name. An escort took us up to the courtroom where my trial was to take place. I sat on the prosecutor's side and waited. I was a little nervous because it was getting late, and Paul and his attorney were nowhere in sight. My mind started going crazy thinking that once again we were going to be delayed or possibly my family was right, maybe Paul took off.

Just as my mind was really starting to go crazy, the courtroom door opened and in walked Paul, his wife, and the attorney. The look on their faces was so clear and cocky that I believe Paul was feeling no fear. He actually looked like, "Let's just get this over with. You're wasting my time". They took their seats on the defense side and waited.

The judge addressed several small cases before ours. It was rather interesting to observe how the judge handled these cases. He seemed very fair and gave people the benefit of the doubt.

Once the other cases were settled, our names were called. The judge asked if everyone was present and ready to proceed with the trial. All agreed, but my attorney had some other motions to file, one of them being the submission of the allegations I accused Paul of when we lived up north. Paul's attorney wanted the audiotape to be eliminated from trial. This and other motions were discussed; I was not allowed to attend this portion of the hearing. I sat in the hallway with my mother and waited for the outcome.

About an hour later, my attorney came out with a smile. He said that my testimony from up north would be allowed, that the talk of my teenage sexual activity would not be allowed, and, most importantly to the case, the tapes would be allowed in the trial. YES! I was starting to feel good. This was the first time something had gone right for me. The smug look Paul once had on his face appeared to lessen a little from that defeat. My face, however was feeling a little less tense.

I have to think that Paul was probably wondering where everyone was for my support. Normally when we went to court, I had a group of people with me, but this morning it was just my mother, Karen, and I. I knew, of course, that was soon going to change. Soon that courtroom would be full of supporters.

Now that the ruling was clear that certain damning evidence was going to be allowed, the jury selection was about to begin. When it comes to jury selection, the victim is not allowed to be present, but once again, Paul, the defendant was allowed. Jury selection is a long process taking as long as two to three hours or more. Sitting in the hallway once again with Karen and my mother, we made a lot of small talk, but my mind was on what was going on behind the courtroom doors. My attorney had requested another attorney, a white female to take second chair as did Paul's attorney, and he claimed she was an attorney that worked in his office. She was going to help Paul's attorney pick a jury. After all, she was a woman and would know what to look for.

Finally, the jury selection was made and surprisingly it was all women. I was sure the defense would want at least one or two men on it. Instead, the jury consisted of women ranging in age of approximately 25 to 50 years of age.

Since we had approached the lunch hour, it was time for a recess. We were to resume at 2:00 p.m. My mother, Karen, and I decided to head off to the cafeteria for lunch and conversation while we waited for the others to arrive.

Chapter Twenty-Two – Afternoon of the Trial

Karen treated my mother and me to a nice lunch in the cafeteria. We noticed that Paul and his little group of people were sitting at a table just behind us, not eating anything.

About halfway through our lunch, Sgt. Chris Long walked in. He came right over to the table and gave my mother and me a big hug and kiss on the cheek. He joined us at the table after getting something from the grill. Soon after that, my aunt, two uncles, two cousins, their spouses, my brother and his wife, another victim advocate from the courthouse, and six neighbors of Paul's came in and sat with us. It quickly turned into a friendly gathering, and once again, any fears or nervousness went away. All these people at the table were here for me, and they were here because they believed me and wanted to support me.

I turned around and noticed that Paul only had two neighbors, his wife, her daughter and her son-in-law. Their conversation practically stopped as they watched us. I'm sure Paul was in disbelief that so many people were there for me, when earlier no one but my mother and Karen were present.

While sitting with my family and friends, my attorney advised that he wanted to meet with Chris and me in about twenty minutes. I felt my heart skip a beat, but I was reassured by Chris, Karen, and my mother that everything was going to be okay. I suddenly realized I'd forgotten my angel worry stone that was given to me. Inside the stone was an angel, and I was told to carry it with me and hold it in my hands when I felt scared or just needed a little extra help. I started to panic. My mother reached for her wallet and pulled out a mother/daughter coin that I had once given her to carry. I took it with me to meet with Carl. It turned out to be just a little update on how the rest of the day would play out. Carl was going to do the opening statement and then I would testify. Originally Chris was going to go before me. My testimony would be conducted privately as none of my family or friends wanted to hear me re-live the molestation I endured night after night during my childhood. They thought it would be best to give me that time without the added pressure of upsetting them.

After my testimony we would have a brief recess to give my family and friends the opportunity to enter the courtroom. Then the audiotapes would be played. Once that was done, Chris would testify and then his videotape of the arrest interrogation would be played. At that point, the state would rest and the defense would then present its case.

Following these instructions Karen and I went back to my family. Chris stayed with Carl and his assistant to go over the tapes and video, both of which needed to be edited. Chris would be a part of that process. In addition, Carl's second chair attorney, Denise, would be cross-examining Chris, and she needed to go over his testimony with him.

It was now time for the trial to begin. Carl was in the courtroom with Denise presenting the opening statement. Karen, who I wanted to be in there the whole time, was sitting right up front where she could hear and see everything.

My emotions began to take over. People were hanging close to me, but I suddenly wanted to be alone. I walked over to a corner and looked out the window. I started to cry. My mother came over and comforted me. She helped to "bring me back" by talking to me in her sweet, soft voice, telling me everything was going to be fine and I was going to do great. I really listened to her, and I suddenly stopped crying and found myself gaining strength. We stood by the window together for a few more minutes and then joined everyone in the group outside the courtroom. I told them that when my name was called to go in, I did not, under any circumstances, want anyone saying to me, "Hey Elaine! Good luck," or "Knock em' dead," or "Break a leg." I just wanted to get up and walk in without hearing anything from anyone.

The door opened at that moment, and the bailiff called my name into the hall. I stood up and walked towards the bailiff. Karen was also standing there. We stood between two sets of doors, one from the outside into a tiny hall area and the other leading directly into the courtroom.

I must have looked scared out of my mind because the bailiff put both of his hands on my shoulders, looked me in the eyes and said, "Breathe. You will be fine. Be strong. Go in there and go directly to my co-worker. She will direct you from there. He told me earlier to look at the jury when answering questions, not him. I found myself drawn to one juror in particular; she had a kind face and looked like she was probably a mother.

I did as he instructed. After I was sworn in, I took my seat in the witness box and took a deep breath. My attorney stood next to the juror box so my attention would be directed to the women in the jury and not him. He told me earlier to look at the jury when answering questions, not him. I found myself drawn to one juror in particular; she had a kind face and looked like she was probably a mother.

What is strange is that I don't really remember much about my testimony itself, but I do remember seeing that one juror wiping tears from her eyes. I remember crying and having the judge hand me a tissue. I also remember asking him for a drink of water, which he poured for me.

My attorney was extremely gentle and caring during the difficult questioning. When it was time for Paul's attorney to examine me, I remember feeling calm. A lot of his questions were overruled, and he was told to move on. I didn't think his questioning took that long—maybe ten minutes or less. I found out later I was in there for over an hour. After the interrogation was complete, I got myself upset and all worked up, and went out of the courtroom in a crying rage. I stormed into the bathroom crying out loud that Carl had screwed up and didn't ask me the right questions or enough questions. The judge called a recess, and Karen and Carl came looking for me. Everyone was asking what had happened. My family told Carl that I was very upset and crying. Both Karen and Carl seemed confused and asked everyone what they were talking about. They said that I did awesome; Karen said it was a "slam dunk." Carl, Karen, and my mother met me at the bathroom and right away, Carl hugged me and told me I had done a wonderful job and not to worry. I was relieved and comforted, of course.

Court was back in session and everyone except my mother and I were allowed back into the courtroom where the tapes were played. We weren't allowed into the courtroom because I was the victim and my mother was listed as a potential witness. The sad thing was I guess when I came out of the courtroom all upset I really upset one of the dads named Jack from the neighborhood because he just had tears in his eyes and sat with us. When I asked him if he was going to go in and listen to the rest of the hearing he just said he couldn't and really wanted to stay with my mother and I. I was so glad he did, he really helped to pass the time. Meanwhile back behind closed doors Chris took the stand and his video was played. The court then went into recess before the defense presented its case.

Out in the hallway, everyone filled my mother, me and Jack in on what had happened in the courtroom. Everyone was shocked to hear the tapes. Some of them had heard about them, but no one had ever listened to them. All agreed that the tapes were damaging.

After a short recess it was time for Paul's defense to begin. And once again, everyone except my mother and I went back into the courtroom. The only defense they had to offer was Paul's testimony itself. He decided to take the stand to defend the allegations. According to family and friends, his testimony only made him appear guiltier. That part of the trial didn't seem to take very long because, before I knew it, everyone was coming out saying there was a ten-minute recess before closing arguments would be heard.

I was glad that the major portion of the trial was over. Closing arguments was the only portion of the whole trial that my mother and I were able to attend, so after the recess I entered the courtroom with everyone else and I was instructed to sit in the front row.

Carl began his closing argument, and it was powerful. Everyone on my side of the room was crying, and I do mean everyone, plus several of the jurors were wiping tears or fighting back tears. I was overwhelmed by what was going on. Carl was passionate and direct about his statements. It was easy to feel the emotions that he was giving off. He was brilliant. At this point, I was crying so hard I couldn't breathe. I held my mother's and Karen's hands. Both of them were also crying. This was going to be over soon, and I had to hang in there and be strong.

Finally, Paul's attorney got up and presented his closing arguments. He tried to blame my mother, making statements like "where was the mother while this was going on." This might have been a mistake on their part because other mothers in the jury may have taken exception to the insinuation. Sympathy was not likely to be on Paul's side.

The closing arguments were over, and the judge was giving the jurors last- minute instructions. It was about 8:30 at night and no one had-had dinner yet, so the judge instructed the jurors to go eat the food that was delivered and then start to deliberate for their decision.

We all left the courtroom and went into the hall. Everyone was mentally drained but at the same time feeling pretty good. My uncle decided that he would order pizzas and sodas for everyone since no one could or wanted to leave the courthouse. Paul and his family went downstairs and sat in a dark, closed cafeteria. They didn't eat any dinner; they only ate chips and drank soda from the vending machines.

It was nice to be with everyone, even if it was from the courtroom hallway. Some of us sat on benches while we ate, and others sat on the floor. It was a sight that Chris found incredible, and he said that he had never seen such support in the courtroom before. He kept saying that he wished he had a camera.

Time was passing and it was getting late. Chris had to leave because his wife was flying out of state in the morning and he was taking her to the airport. My uncle from the Carolinas had to leave because of a pre-planned business meeting, and he needed sleep before his long drive home. I walked them both downstairs to the front door. We hugged and kissed and said our good-byes. Both made me promise to call them as soon as the verdict was read. I promised and went back up to the courtroom hallway.

The day had seemed to move right along for me, but this part seemed to drag on. What was going on in there? Did these jurors believe me? What would happen if they didn't? What if they couldn't make a decision? All these things were going through my mind as well as the minds of everyone with me. At this point though, all we could do was wait.

Chapter Twenty-Three – The Verdict Is In

About 11:00 that night the courtroom doors opened and a bailiff stepped into the hallway. "The jury is in and we have a verdict" rang through the long, dark hallway. Everyone stood up and just looked at each other. We all hugged, but no one did a lot of talking. As I stood up, my legs felt wobbly, and I wasn't sure I was going to be able to make the walk into the courtroom.

Once inside, I sat in the front row with my mother on one side of me and Karen on the other. Our group took up three rows in the courtroom, and we all were bonded together as we held hands. I was so nervous, I was shaking and tears were rolling down my face faster than I could wipe them away. Paul and his group were also sitting in the courtroom; Paul sat with the attorneys and his small group sat behind him. The judge came in and we all stood. After being told to sit down, he began a small lecture to everyone in the room. He said that we had a lot of work to do here and outbursts would not be tolerated. Once the verdict was read, he did not want to hear any outbursts of emotion of any type from either side, whether the verdict was good or bad. With that said, the jury was brought back in.

"I understand that you the jury have reached a verdict. Is that correct?" asked the judge.

"Yes, your honor that is correct," responded the madam floor person.

"Please hand your verdict to the bailiff." The bailiff handed the piece of paper that held my future and Paul's to the judge's assistant. "If you would please read the verdict out loud to the court," instructed the judge.

At this point, I couldn't breathe. My heart was beating so fast, I could feel it in my throat. As the assistant was opening the paper, my ears felt like they were plugging up. I couldn't hear anything. Everything seemed to move in slow motion. I kept looking at my mother, and she had the same blank look in her eyes. I found out later her ears were doing the same thing. This woman was reading the verdict, and I couldn't make out what she was saying.

I looked around at the others in our group. All of them were crying, but they all had slight smiles on their faces. My sister-in-law was nodding her head. At that point, I figured the verdict had to be in my favor. I do remember vaguely hearing, "In the charge of capital sexual battery to a child under the age of 12, we the jury find the defendant, Paul Carole, guilty." I didn't know what to do. I was being slammed with all these emotions, and I couldn't believe it was over. Karen was crying just as hard as I. She was such a great support system, not only to me but with everyone in the group as well.

The judge thanked the jury and then dismissed them. At that point, the judge asked if there was any reason why sentencing shouldn't take place. Paul's attorney responded: "Not any legal reason, Your Honor." Of course, my attorney nodded in agreement to proceed. The judge instructed Paul to stand. He then asked my attorney what type of sentence he was seeking.

"Your Honor, we feel we have no other choice than to request that this man be sentenced to life in prison with no chance of parole for twenty-five years," Carl said.

During the long pause after Carl's request, I noticed that the jury had come back into the courtroom and was sitting behind me. They wanted to hear the outcome.

The judge then spoke. "Mr. Carole, the audiotapes that were heard here today were extremely incriminating. I have no choice but to sentence you here today to spend the rest of your natural life in prison with no chance of parole for twenty-five years. Sir, what you did to your daughter was a crime; it is a crime that no child should ever have to experience. Is there anything you would like to say, sir?" asked the judge.

For a moment it appeared that Paul was going to say something but his attorney whispered something into his ear and his somber response was just "No Your Honor."

Paul's attorney then asked the judge if it would be okay if Paul hugged his wife good-bye. The judge agreed but said they each had to stay on their side of the little half wall. The jury then got up and left, and the others in my group then followed. I wanted so badly to thank them for finding him guilty, so my mother and I got up to walk out with everyone else. Just as I got up, however, Karen told my mother and me to sit back down and watch the rest of the process. The three of us sat back in our seats. After Paul hugged his wife, he was then escorted near a door that was right in front of me. Before going through the door, he was instructed to remove his dress coat, tie, belt, the pen in his pocket, and his wallet. The bailiff then handed all of these belongings to his wife who was crying out of control. Before handing off the wallet, he opened it up and took out two five-dollar bills and put them in his pocket. He then turned to walk through the door. When he reached for the door handle, the bailiff told him to back away from the door. Karen commented that Paul would never again be able to open any door for himself.

After Paul was gone, I walked out of the courtroom. Carl was standing there with the biggest, most beautiful smile on his face. We hugged one another for what seemed like forever. It was the best feeling ever. He whispered in my ear, "You did it," and I whispered back, "We did it." Everyone in my group hugged me and then hugged Carl as if he was one of the family.

We were instructed that we needed to leave the building and parking area immediately. As we walked to our cars, I called my uncle and told him the great news. He was so happy for me. I then called Chris. When I told him the verdict, I could hear the overwhelming joy in his voice.

The women from the neighborhood told me that they spoke to the jury before they left and expressed our sincere thanks to each of them. They also had a question they wanted answered. They wanted to know why Chris Long contacted me after all this time. One of the women said it was because Paul had sexually molested a few of the children in the neighborhood. They said they were glad they made the right decision. They had a strong feeling that there was something more to this that they were not privileged to hear. Carl was right. They were listening.

Everyone got into their cars and headed home. It had been a very long day, and I was mentally exhausted. When my mother and I arrived home, we changed clothes and sat together on the couch. We exchanged stories about what we were feeling when the verdict was read and then when the judge declared sentence. Both of us had figured that the sentence would take place another day; it was a surprise to both of us that it was completed the same day.

That night was the best night's sleep I'd had in a long time. For once, I had sweet dreams and no fears at all. The next day, I felt like a new person and it was wonderful. It was early and the phone started ringing off the wall, it was the children from Paul's neighborhood, they were all calling me to thank me for setting *them* free and giving there neighborhood back to them. Apparently one of older gentlemen went shopping later that day and bought all his neighbor kids side walk chalk, for the first time in a long time these kids were going to get to do what kids do best…play and have fun in the front yard once again.

Before the trial started, Karen had wanted to know if I wanted the media to cover the case. I was not comfortable with that idea since I was still trying to protect my family. Having it broadcasted all over the news was not what I wanted. I did agree, however, to contact the gentleman from the newspaper that wrote the first article. I spent a lot of time with this person, and the article was wonderful. It covered everything from the children in the neighborhood to my stolen childhood to the final victory. The editor thought this story was so powerful that it was put on the front page and then continued onto another page on the biggest paper sale day…Sunday.

The article prompted calls to come in to the police station and attorney's office with words of praise. Someone even wrote a letter to the paper, which was later, printed in the "Opinion" section praising everyone involved. Having this article printed and received with such positive feedback was just the closure I needed. I knew I could move on, and life would be good.

Final Thoughts

As I mentioned earlier, this book was written to share with others the fears I have lived all my life. The funny thing is I really wasn't aware of them because I had lived with it day after day. To me this was "normal."

Being molested or raped night after night by a person that should have been protecting me is a horrible thing. As an adult now, I realize all the wonderful things I missed as a child. I always had to be "on guard." I couldn't just be a kid and have the free mind of a child. Instead, I needed to protect my brother from this horrible violation and protect my mother from the threats that were whispered in my ear on a regular basis.

For too many years I let this man ruin me, even after I moved out he still was controlling me. I had little or in most case no self-respect. I didn't care that men saw me as a sure thing; I did a lot of reckless things to myself, drinking, smoking pot, having sex with whoever showed me a little attention. I know I can't blame everything bad that has happened to me in my life on this man, but I believe I was self-destructive to myself because of him. Today, this is no longer the case; it is time for me to take care of me. I know that I am important and worth a lot more than I thought…no one will ever take my self-worth and respect from me again.

I also learned another thing during this whole process, when I was sharing with Chris my story I was blaming myself for the horrible things Paul did to the children in his neighborhood, deep down I know I was not to blame, I was once one of those children and I was afraid. The families in the neighborhood don't blame me for what happened and I have learned to not blame myself, Paul was the adult here…not me and not the children in his neighborhood. We are all told growing up to respect adults and listen to them, now we need to teach our children that it is okay to tell on an adult that is hurting us and doing something wrong…and molesting children is wrong. Don't let words that are being whispered into your ear at night keep you from doing what you know you should do…tell someone, get your life back or help someone you know that told you as a secret, help them get there life back. People out there will believe you…you just have to believe in yourself and stop for the first time in your life and no longer be the frightened little child like I was for all these horrible years.

I hope this also convinces everyone that our judicial system really does work. I learned that it may not move as quickly as we would like, or at times, it may not seem fair, but in the end it does work. The world is full of wonderful people like Chris, Karen and Carl. You just have to believe and be patient and let the system run its course. I lived it and now understand it.

During the case and trial, I was referred to as "the victim." I guess I never thought of myself as a victim, but for the first time in my life, it was okay to let my guard down and let someone else protect me. That was a nice feeling; it was something that I never felt, since I was always the protector.

In the courtroom, when Karen made the comment that Paul would never be able to open a door again for himself, it really didn't register or have much meaning to me at the time. That night, when I went to my bedroom, my door was closed. As I put my hand on the doorknob, I realized that no one would ever be able to open my door again at night and hurt me the way Paul did all those years. Thanks to a great system I can look at Paul by going on to the states prison system website and see for myself this monsters mug shot and take the virtual tour of the prison. As sick as this may sound…I get great pleasure doing this. The state also offers a great added comfort to "victims," I am on a calling system whereas if Paul moves to another prison for any reason, or god forbid escapes I am notified right away. I was notified when he was moved to a state facility. This extra protection is very comforting and helps me to rest better at night.

About a week after the case, while brushing my teeth, as I looked at myself in the mirror, I realized that I was no longer a victim. I was "ME." What a wonderful feeling! I felt like a new person. I felt like I'd been released from prison. In a sense, I had been in prison all my life, but someone's huge force found the key to let me out and I could breathe again.

If something like this is happening to you or to someone you know, don't have the attitude I did and think that if I can survive, then they will, too because deep down you are not surviving you are still that frightened child and the other person is really depending on you to help them, and, you may hold the vital key to her, or his, prison door.

You don't have to be a victim all of your life. Tell someone now so you can start living your life once again without fear.

Update

Since writing this experience Paul has filed several appeals with the court. All of which were denied, except one. In 2006 he appealed to the court that his original attorney was incompetent and that compelling evidence was never brought to trial that would have showed the jury that he was innocent and I was lying.

The court granted him a hearing to see if there was indeed enough evidence to warrant a new trial. Of course this brought up a lot of old emotions and fears. Even though the attorney assigned to the case, family, Chris, Karen and others all told me over and over that this monster was not going to be granted a new trial...but never say never right??

This time I was able to sit in on the court proceedings and to see this monster in his orange prison jumpsuit which raised a lot of unsettling fears. I couldn't believe he was doing it to me again...what did this monster have over me? How could he still have this much control over me? I have to give him this, he is good, and he could still look at me and make me feel like I was seven years old again.

I sat in silence and listened to his attorney, to the state attorney and testimony both from Paul and then from his original attorney that he was now suing. I was ill. I couldn't believe the things I was hearing...again Paul was lying and telling everyone in the courtroom that I was the one that started this "relationship" with him. I wanted to vomit, I wanted to scream and had such an urge to jump out of my seat and physically hurt him. Did these people really believe him?

When the testimony was done the judge did not render a verdict that day, he instructed each attorney to put the closing arguments in writing by a certain deadline and then we would come back for the verdict a month later.

When we left the courtroom I really felt and believed that once again this monster was going to get his way. Others still believed that nothing was going to change, or were they just telling me that so I would feel better?

I called the attorney the day after the deadline to see if she submitted her closing arguments and to see just how she felt this case was going to go. She expressed over and over again to me that she was going to win this fight. I wanted to badly to believe her, but my gut was just not feeling as confident.

About a week later I got a call from the state attorney's office, Jennifer the attorney said that in her hand was the verdict from the judge. He felt it would have been a waste of time and taxpayers money to bring the prisoner back for the verdict so he went ahead and rendered his decision in writing. We won!!! The defense did not prove there was anything wrongful during the trial that would have changed the outcome.

I of course cried with relief and then called everyone I knew to share our victory again. It's like a lot of the people involved in this case stated, "Wouldn't you appeal all you could if you were sitting in a 6x9 cell everyday with nothing better to do?" I guess they are right, what else does Paul have to live for? Twenty-five years to life is a long time when you are only in your mid-sixties...I guess I would do the same thing.

Again the system showed that I do have rights and it is here to protect me. I am happy to say that I living life to the fullest, for the second time I am feeling free and full of life.

I am now sharing my story with others in schools, advocate meetings and other organizations. It is fulfilling and meaningful to me to know that I may be helping others by sharing my story. If I even touch one person listening to me, I know then by coming forward it was the right thing to do...and I am making a difference.